Reflections from a Rocking Chair

An Anthology of Jerry's New & Favorite Poems

By Jerry Siegel

Reflections from a Rocking Chair

Cover by Jacob Kubon

Printed in the United States of America

ISBN 978-1-939294-79-1

Published by

Splattered Ink Press

Dedicated to Angie and Jack.

Acknowledgments

After eight decades of life, with families raised and bucket lists often finished or nearing completion, most of us begin a process of reflecting on the life we have lived. We may ruminate about the challenges, successes, and opportunities it has provided to us, and wonder if it has given us everything, we really thought life should provide. Sitting and slowly rocking in a chair can provide clarity for what our life has meant to not only ourselves but to others.

Many of us realize that we are a collection of the thoughts and ideas of the communities who have shared our life journey. As a poet, I found I write short stories, some called poems. The selection and collection of poems in this book were determined by including poems that readers especially enjoyed, and shared comments with me about.

I am exceedingly grateful to the many people who took the time to personally let me know they enjoyed a particular poem! That encouragement kept me writing. So, thank you to each of you. I tried to pass that same encouragement forward to my students.

And finally, I must acknowledge my most amazing wife, who has helped me in every area of getting this book to the printer. We shared the stories of our lives for the world to see, always trying to make this world a better and happier place. For that, I am forever grateful! Get yourself a rocking chair and enjoy a few poems!

Thanks for joining me ..... Jer

Table of Contents

Meditation Whispers
Chapter One

A Path Toward Mediation

Decluttering life,
home, mind and
social affairs
often gives a person
more room to breathe and
less to worry about

Minimalism presents a path
toward refocusing
giving time and space for
mediation

Getting rid of psychological and
physical excessive stuff
makes room in our
physical dwellings and
mental space to
feel fresh air as
new areas are opened

It often replaces
stagnant thoughts
carried by
old age and
out of date habits
antiquated ways of living
that may burden us down

With possessions gone
we are no longer owned by
their memories and
the control they
once held over our
thoughts and minds

Mediation can now
gain a foothold
and begin calming stress and
healing inner emptiness
helping us find
meaningful purposefulness
for our lives

A Poem About Nothing

I'm thinking about writing a poem
About nothing

Or about everything

However, people who know nothing
aren't very astute

And
People who know everything can be
very obnoxious

Maybe nothing isn't a good topic
For a poem
And everything is just too much
For a poem

Yet it seems I should write about
Something!
Something seems manageable
But I am conflicted

What some "thing" do I write about

Maybe "Thing" is the problem
Readers would wonder what
Thing
I was writing about

I guess this now really is a
Poem about nothing!

Everything will have to wait
Because
I have nothing to write about.

Heaven is Getting Closer

I guess being in my 70s
moves me closer to the pearly gates than
having pearly white teeth

It seems every month or two
a good friend will
hop the train to heaven

The friends I still have
are walking more slowly
a few can no longer play sports
so many are using hearing aids
I may have to learn ASL

When we go out to eat
they forget their billfolds or
forgot to load them with cash before they leave
some are wearing fancy pants without pockets

The main topics of conversation are
who takes the most pills
who has the youngest doctors and
who snagged a handicapped license for their cars

Some argue about whether heaven
will have Buffet or table service
(I'm thinking Buffets especially
for those who will get their "just desserts")

Me ......
I'm worried about remembering
which gate I'm supposed to use to
get into heaven!

In the Now

I was waiting for tomorrow
to return some things from yesterday

It was then I realized I
was spending too much time
thinking about yesterday and tomorrow

The moment I am in
Gives meaning to
yesterday, today and tomorrow

the now
is really the center of everything

it's in the now
I can feel myself breathing deeply

It's in the now
I can write words which escape time
Remembering the joys and wonder of yesterday

It's in the now
I can plan for the excitement and hope of tomorrow

It's in the now I can think of
You my friend and fellow companion

It's in the now I can walk and talk with you
about life

It's in the now I can appreciate life.

Letting Go of Sports

I loved water skiing
jumping waves
slalom
Skiing bare foot
starting from the dock
Now I fear falling and
the water is getting harder!

I reveled in downhill skiing
adrenalin pumping
track left, track right
blue and black star trails
moguls
now I stick to the bunny hills and
do a lot of snowplowing!

I indulged in competitive tennis
three hour matches
singles, doubles
trophies
now I play for exercise and
not very hard at that

I used to enjoy backpacking
two three weeks at a time
pitching my tent at night

cooking over a small tin can
now a half hour walk
with the grand kids calls for a nap!

Golf was my passion
driving that little ball far down the fairway
seeing it sink into the cup
now my frustration far outweighs the enjoyment
when my drives dribble down
the fairway and my putts land
inches from the cup.

I'm not sure whether I let go of sports
or they let go of me
I still walk to the mail box to get the mail and
take the garbage out
do they count as a sports?

Life's Journey

In life
We like to share our thoughts
that wander and change as we age
usually living within lines and boundaries
we set years ago

Then one day we find mellifluous music
swelling from the recesses of our soul
demanding to be heard

Each year we live
we continue to find new
Motivation and purpose
giving passion to our journey

We find new interpretations in moments lived
realizing our
lives are a beautiful work in progress

When we reach our final destination
our life will become a complete story
a finished composition
remembered by
those
who loved
us most

Little Lights

Little lights help me meditate
I love little lights
On Christmas trees
Candles in frosted windows
Flashlights in pup tents
Soft lights in church
Twinkling stars
Campfires in the woods
Reading books by flashlight
Dim lights in halls

Little lights
With beam so small
Say come sit with me
My spirit is yours
To nourish and hold

I find God in little lights
He too shares
Love and warmth
In the littlest of the
Heavenly body's

Mediation Song

Many activities have their own
Voice and language
Sports have
cheers and fight songs
Weddings have
words of commitment and love songs
Funerals have
Memorials and songs of heaven
The military have
marching and victory songs

Meditation also has it's own
voice and song

It is the way words are voiced that
take us to our special mediation place of
silence and solitude so we
can hear our soul quietly speaking

The hymn writers got it right
when they wrote
"Whisper a prayer in the morning,
Whisper a prayer at noon
Whisper a prayer in the evening
To keep your heart in tune"

Mediation is an emotion
a whisper
a quiet song that
unlocks our heart and soul
and allows us to
listen to our inner voice.

Mediation Whispers

Mediation often arrives with a
gentle whisper

A coffee pot's subdued perking
In the early morning
A distant train's haunting whistle
On a moonlight night

A woodpecker tapping on a hollow tree
In the chilly autumn,
The creaking of a rocking chair
While comforting a child

Beautiful majestic music
Enjoyed in a comfy chair
Fire in the hearth while reflecting
On a loved ones smile

Water dripping from a canoe paddle
On the first spring outing,
A distant loon calling
At summer's end

Seagulls rising high on
unseen thermals
A barefoot walk on
sandy beaches

We are often surrounded by
These meditative whispers that
caress the moments we are in
They calm our life,
Still our heart and
Soothe our souls

We gently hold these moments in
grateful solitude
They guide our spirit toward
Serenity and peace

my mediation

i gently close my eyes
shutting out the world of
sounds around me
listening to the rhythm and
quiet beating of my heart

i breath slowly
filling my lungs fully
trying to relax slowly from my
toes to my sunburned forehead

it's then and only then
my mind releases
worries - anxieties - fears - even expectations
now i'm feeling free

i wander like a contented traveler
down paths in pastoral surroundings
walk on sunny beaches

I feel my soul being refreshed
my spirit being lifted
like a pelican on a rising thermal

in this moment I'm one with the world and
at peace with the universe

Rocking Chair

There's something about the gentle motion
Of a rocking chair
That Gently taps into the shadows
Of our memories

It lets us relive briefly
Time and thoughts
We had while being cradled in it arms

We feel the weight of a child
Falling asleep against our breast

We remember tiredness leaving our bodies
After a long day of work

We recall comforting a little one who
was upset over a bruised a knee

We recollect reading a good book by the fire
on a chilly winter night

Now we rest in that comfy, creaky old chair
slowly rocking and

thinking of the life we have lived
Lulled back into remembering our

Wonderful life's journey
And thanking God for our many blessings

The Ocean

On my birthday week
I want to sit
By the ocean
And watch the waves

They've kept track of
The years I've lived
Of all the times I've
Walked in their undulating waters

These waves were there through
My joys and my sorrows
They've felt my emotions

The white foam between
My toes was solace to my soul
It's many colors a reflection of
My feelings

The ocean waves
Know how to touch my
Spirit and soul
It brings me peace

For the journey
That lies a head
I count the days

I know you ocean friend
Together we shall
Share eternity !

The Train

Today we built new steps
on the back of a
small and tiny house
for an elderly lady

her back steps
were crumbling

As we worked
I realized
that railroad tracks
ran very close to the house

In an in-between moment
I walked off the distance
between house and track
forty-two feet

I thought about all the trains
coming down that track
shaking and rumbling through
this frail ladies house

goldfish bouncing in the bowl
pictures jumping on the wall
dishes rattling on the shelves
could she hear the engineers talking

why did she live so close to the tracks
was it the only house available
maybe her husband long past
worked for the c & o
the steps are repaired,
Now
she waits for the next train

I Need to Laugh
Chapter two

Angels at Ocean Village

Where do angels
Hang out at Ocean Village

I know they hover and
Sweep low to the ground
Avoiding the new walls
That keep the trespassers out

They always touch the needy
Help the poor
They support the down and out

They walk among us
Seeking - watching for
Kindness in word and deed

I think I met one
Yesterday
She asked about
My golf game

Golf, I said, is such peaceful game

Yes she said
God is tired of war and strife
He just took up golf and
Finds it's relaxing

I told the angel
That if God got a hole in one
He'd have to buy drinks
For for every one

And in a moment
Of humorous relief
She said, even the Republicans?

Now I know God is real!
Drinks for all of
Us here on the big blue marble!

That's going to cost
A hell of a lot!!!

Jer

Brussel sprouts

Some people smell
And so do Brussel sprouts
I know they are
good for you
I'm told they
Clean the intestinal tract
In just one setting

They don't look too bad
Charred brown on the edges
When cooked upon the grill
However they still have a strong smell

My wife doesn't allow me to cook them in the house
(I'm relegated to the charcoal grill)
And lights scented candles right and left
When I do

I'm trying to think of some animals who'd like
Brussel sprouts
Maybe alligators in the swamp
Or skunks

I don't think they'll have smelly
Brussels' sprouts in heaven
But I'm sure they'll have crispy
McDonald's French fries
And maybe even onion rings

Feeling Smart

When I get two or three questions
On jeopardy correct
I feel a tad bit smart

Once in a while
I nail 5 or 6 questions
I start to cough trying to tune in
my spouse that I'm feeling smart

I Bring up topics like
remember when we were in Philosophy
class together
Remember professor Matthews
What are the rings around Saturn
Made of

I Start feeling lighted headed
Nail one more question
Who came up with
The Socratic method
I am riding so high

Then my spouse asks me,
"Did you pick up
The milk I asked you to get
For dinner tonight"

I say, "Tom our next neighbor
Just texted me.
I will be right back"
I grab my keys on the
way out the door

Flurries of Greatness

After turning 75 I had to decide
on a new path for enjoying
competitive sports

my old friends are now
retiring from physical activity
so I have to play with
younger folks who are
surpassing me in
so many areas and yet
I still love athletics

Realizing I still had
moments of diminishing greatness
I now play for the camaraderie
and exercise

I no longer have the low score in golf
however there is that
unexpected birdie and
an ace in tennis from nowhere that
gives me an adrenaline surge

Flurries of greatness I call them
I'm squeezing out joy and happiness
every day
and occasionally a winner's beer
Life is still beautiful at 75

Friday Night at the Retirement Village

We struggled trying to decide
What our date night dinner should be
Was the chicken salad from Wednesday too old?
What could we make from four brown bananas?

Were the left overs from
last Sunday or Monday?
Looks like crunchy fish
Or it could be quesadillas
Which one had the delightful green sauce on it?

We both knew we needed fiber so
Maybe beans and brats for dinner
I see a bag of salad behind the
unopened bag of mushy carrots

We settled on Special K cereal with almonds
With some fiber gummy's and
Red wine for dessert

I tuned to Marty Robbins for romance an
We ended up watching Jeopardy

Friday nights are special in the retirement village

Kids and Hammocks!

Today my grandchildren,
Received their new Hammocks
From amazon.com

I watched their joy in
Tying their hammock to the trees

The delight in getting in and
falling out of these hanging beds

There were many hours of
Laughter and fun in those hammocks

It then occurred to me
If God wants these wonderful
children to come up
and join the saints in heaven

She will need trees that are spaced 12 foot a part

So blessed angels who are waiting for us to arrive
Instead of paving the streets of gold

plant tons of trees

Do you have hammocks up there
Or shall
The kids bring their own?

I'm Happy

Exactly when in a day
Am I happy?

I like getting up
Stepping on the scale
And see I've lost
a half pound
I'm happy!

Oatmeal for breakfast?
Nope
French toast with
crispy bacon
Now that makes me happy

Coffee @ 10:30 without a sweet
is sad, but an
apple fritter with coffee
Makes me oh so happy!

A salad for lunch is
Probably healthy but
A French dip sandwich with
fries make me smile from ear to ear
Yes happy!

At happy hour
Carrots and celery

Makes me feel like a rabbit but
Fish dip with pita chips now
That's reward for a hard days work and
Makes me very happy!

For dinner a Caesar salad with chicken
Screams weight watchers but
A steak and loaded baked potato
Fills me with joy and happiness

Then there's my late hour snack
A Diet Coke and a piece of fruit
It's ok, but a
Slice of Cold Pizza with an IPA beer
Says today I've lived a happy life

Now as I get a tum and crawl
Into bed next to my ultra thin wife whose
Been eating tofu and 4 cal wafers all day
I'm trying to think which part of the day
Was the best!

My Tomorrows are Yesterday

I'm walking slowly toward the finish line
my eyes are getting suspect

Now I call most of the tennis balls out
Before they hit the ground!

I think the white 150 markers on the golf course
Are the 200 yard markers

Golf Ponds 30 yards out seem
Like Lake Michigan on a stormy day

I look for my wallet when the restaurant bill comes
But there's too many pockets in these my shorts
Can't seem to find it ....

I discover seniors don't celebrate
Happy hour just early dinner specials

I wonder if I wore these same clothes yesterday?
If I put them in the hamper I wouldn't
have to worry about that

I'm trying to remember If I complemented
the lovely lady at the golf shack

Did I say, "Do you tweet" or
Or "you are sweet"

I'm wishing today was yesterday
For then I was wearing a new shirt
And looking GOOD!

Pickle Ballers

I love being around pickle ballers
The last several years
I think they have earned their own special
Gate into the streets of gold

Tennis players earned their pass
Through the pearly gates
With sophisticated rules

They won't even let their
players get away with a foot being at fault
They also call a let when they mean
no let - do it over

Pickle ballers talk about a ladder
They have to climb
Only there's no actual ladder

They tell you to stay out of the kitchen
But there is no actual kitchen

Any sport that involves a paddle
Has to be a great motivator
Especially to wayward grandkids

Pickle ball has certainly
Helped us live longer

And yes I think there will be pickle ball
In heaven

I've seen folks down here playing in sandals
Maybe they were getting ready to
play pickle ball up there

SENIOR Golf

Today with aging friends
We whacked golf balls
Bouncing some off condos
Splashing many in the ponds
Some into sandy bunkers

To distract us from our wayward shots
We talked about
The great weather
How great our last game was
Even Bar Mitzvah recipes
All the while hoping we had enough
Pond balls to finish our game

And finally on the ninth
Said a quiet prayer
For one truly good
last shot
it sprayed into the sandy bunker

It's then we hoped that
somewhere in the great unknown
someone else's golf game was
just as bad as our was today !

What time did you want to
Play tomorrow?

Golf and Heaven

In heaven
Betting on golf
Everyone wins
No penalties for missed shots
All balls skip over water hazards

The poorer players are heroes up there
Unlike on earth where those
Given gifts could lord over
The counting of prize money

Those who have yet to win this season
Think it's just another $5 donation
That's not what golf in heaven is all
about

Folks who get a hole in one actually
Tithe on the winnings
In heaven simple folk will
Win over the elites

However for now
Here at Gator Trace or Island Pines
We just hope to have our name
Selected with Bill, Dick or Jim
Paul and Jerry not so much

One more game with Bob P.
We'd all love and cherish forever
From the red tees of course !!

Yesterday
Chapter Three

Amanda

She gathered thoughts from
my mind
and my heart
that I knew were there
but didn't know how to express
and was hesitant to say

She pointed me
in the direction of
light
of what was
right

This skinny little
black girl
telling me
with all my
white privilege
to be brave

So now I want to walk
in harmony with
Her
and you
until my days are done
and truly be
that light.

Together

Sometimes the
Quality of the moment
We are living in is
All we want from the universe

We feel the wonder of our
Own survival
touching
sensing beauty and
tranquility in nature

A host of fellow travelers
share our motivation
To be fully alive in
this moment

With people we love
Who have gone on before
a deep sense of peace overcomes us

At times we may feel ourselves stumble
And reach out to fellow travelers
Life's purpose is found ideally
In walking and being together
Supporting one another

Flowers

A beautiful surprise
when brought
in by a four-year-old
from the flower box
facing the road

A beautiful connection affirmed
when given to a friend
on a job well done or
a life well lived

However I
think flowers were
created to be given from
one lover to another

They seem to best show the wonder
and beauty of love
better than any other gift

Maybe that's why every spring
God fills our world with
beautiful flowers

Golfing With Friends

In January, February, and March
I play golf with you
my Florida friends

"Holiday golf" on Wednesdays
men's social on Thursdays

each of you make our
life's journey
more fun
enjoyable and worthwhile

we agonizing over shots
fuss about bunkers that are unbelievably large
bristle over putts that hang on the edge of the hole

as we golf we slip in a few jokes
share life stories
have a hot dog and beer or two
brag about our beautiful wives and
exceptional grandchildren

we bask in the beautiful sunshine
warm weather seems so surreal in winter
I swear I see many of us thanking God while walking the
course

for just allowing us to live in this moment
in this one beautiful day
the finale holes are are coming
will the "press" come into play!
and God - if you play -
should I uses a six or a seven iron?

Ocean Village

I'm in heaven
Exquisite grounds
Flowers and blooming trees abound
Congenial people all around saying
"Good morning! "
"How are you?"
Outstanding weather
Bright and sunny every day
Scrumptious food, famous chefs
Mouthwatering fish and savory steaks

New restaurants to explore
The Braford Steak house and Taco Azteca
Abundant sports
Tennis, golf and pickle ball to name a few

I hear the ocean roar as I enter sleep
TV, internet, & news are quiet until I chose
Conversations to make me think
Trying to self-actualize

I reminisce and explore with folks from
Arizona, NY and Ontario
Every need met described in my life's goals
Bucket list and surpassed

However I send out a call to
My home in the north
My soul and my heart need to return

To cloudy days
A robin and chipmunk or two
Trips to the mailbox
Puttering in the yard
And dreams of living at OV in sunshine
And talking with you

Hotdogs

Grandpa What is so special about hotdogs?

People will often say bring some hotdogs.
They never say bring some sweaty cats
Or steaming gerbils

Are cool dogs not welcome?
And what about wiener dogs,
Are they a hotdog with just a different name?

How did the dogs get hot the first place?
Had they been running?
Why not cool them off a bit by giving them a shower?

The last thing a person should do
is put an overheated dog
in a warm bun for gosh sakes!

It's silly to put onions on an overheated dog
Then smother it with relish and mustard!
A tub of ice water seems the most humane thing to do

So if someone says get me a hotdog
I would look in the fridge
I bet that's where they go to cool off

Grandpa can you tell some stuff about clown fish
that should be funny!

How to make a "Jerry" Pie

In a large bowl, empty a whole package of Siegel boys

Add
Latest cars
Pretty girls
Unique golf swings
Religious schools and holy scrip-ture
God fearing parents

Stir in a cup of competitive juices and a healthy wedge of hormones.

Mix in a measure of either Amazing Grace sung low and in harmony with Rosalie,

A triumphant lullaby or a slow verse of Oh Happy Day.
Or put in all three!

Stir with a large circle of inclusive colors, sizes and ages of humanity to add a spicy flavor.

In a separate bowl whip up the continuous service from HRS, Habitat for Humanity to over tipping at the tiki.
Carefully chop small cubes of divergent, creative, random thoughts or "we coulds".
(If available wear an apron. These may shoot in any direction and can get messy!

Fold in chocolate bits of inquiry

Add questions that have no answers
Look behind metaphorical trees for shadows of mystery and magic

(Keep a spray can of Mary Jo handy in case
there is smoke or flames)

Bake in the 80° Florida sun with salt filled mist from the ocean surf

Serve in hot tub with Angie and Jack
Have ice cream and cool whip handy

Optional: Read a verse from *Walking Home* to quiet the soul.

By Bill Holliday

I Miss the Moss

Today I walked
The old and worn paths
into the remembrance garden
the old and tired stones
had been repaired and refreshed
Power washed

I miss the worn old dirty stones
but most of all the
soft green moss that
grew thick into
every crack
framing each tired brick

I loved the way it clung between
the bricks
it was cool like felt angel slippers on bare feet and
reminding me of all the wonderful people
who had walked these paths before

But time moves on
even for the moss

The Flu

Oh boy
It knocked me down
Kicked my my tush

I was so weak
I couldn't remember
What I did yesterday

I tried drinking soup
Coughed and coughed
Didn't want food

I prayed for tomorrow to come
It came and the
the flu was still with me

My doctors gave me meds
The flu laughed
And made me cough all the more

I think the flu is evil

After a $700 Doctor Bill
And four different kinds of pills
I think I'm getting back to normal

My daughter asked me if I had a flu shot?
I remember the
shingles shot,
Tetanus shot,
Pneumonia shot
But flu shot?

maybe I forgot!
I think from now on I will give
the flu a little more respect

Next year I'll be in line at Walgreens early
August 1
standing in line with the old folks
Waiting for my flu shot

Traveling Home

Tomorrow I will not be
with thee
Enjoying sun drenched days
Golf and tennis filled days
Shorts and flip-flop relaxing days

I will travel north and join with those
Who now watch icicles
slowly drip Into extinction
Yearn and watch out
frost covered windows for
green blades of grass to emerge

Wherever we abide
We may all drink the same wine
And cherish each marvelous new day
In different ways
However in our hearts
We all feel life swiftly passing
One brief day at a time.

When Am I Most Happy

Exactly when in a day
am I most happy?

I like getting up
Stepping on the scale
Seeing I've lost a half pound

Oatmeal for breakfast
Makes me grumpy
French toast
With crispy bacon
Makes me happy

Coffee without a sweet @ 10:30 is OK
An apple fritter for coffee break
Makes me oh so happy

A salad for lunch
I know I'll get through the day
A French dip with fries
makes me smile from ear to ear
So happy!

At happy hour
Carrots and celery
makes me feel like a rabbit
Fish dip with pita chips

I feel I am being rewarded for
a good days work

For dinner a Caesar salad with chicken
Makes me think of Weight Watchers
A steak and loaded baked potato
fills me with joy and happiness
I'd even share a bit with my partner

Then there's the late evening hour snack
a Diet Coke and a piece of fruit
I know I need something more substantial
cold pizza perhaps with an IPA beer
puts a perfect end to the day.

Now as I get a TUM and
crawl next to my ultra thin sleeping wife
who ate tofu and 4 cal wafers all day
I'm trying to think which part of the day
made me happiest
I want to enjoy tomorrow too!

Covid

Chapter Four

Corona's Still Here

Seems like we've been quarantined
For half our life
Everyone is depressed
Covid flat we call our grim mood
We all trudge on under
its dark foreboding cloud
Moving through life
On automatic pilot
Pandemics have insidious
Ways of dampening the human spirit

However there's a sliver of light
Maybe a vaccination
Is in our near future
If prayers alone could solve
This pandemic,
Millions have already been sent
A tired nation and world
Whispers in every free moment
Please let it be true!

This is a virus we will never forget

Covid Christmas

I was a tiny bit happy
With thoughts of a virtual
Christmas this year

We could avoid the ubiquitous
Christmas parties
No white elephant gifts
Savings on presents for our
Progeny and other relatives

I told the grand kids this
Year I might just hold up
pictures of gifts I
thought they'd like
Santa probably wouldn't be able visit
Quarantine and all

Us old folks could sleep in this year

The Grand Kids wouldn't hear of it!
They skipped arguing and
Jumped right to
hissy fits
They fussed and complained
Put together their own legal case
They quoted mental health experts
Dr Phil, the Constitution and even the Bible
"they came bearing gifts "

So this year on Christmas Eve
If you see an old man in an hazmat suit
dropping off gifts
It's probably just a grandpa
Placating his grandchildren.

At least He didn't have to learn how to zoom!

Covid Vocabulary

COVID-19
Corona-virus
Vaccinations
Quarantine
A-symptomatic
CDC
Underlying symptoms
Anti-vaccination
endEmic
Epidemic
Outbreak
Pandemic
Cluster
Community spread
Transmission
Incubation period
Intubation
Droplet transmission
Super spreader
Flattening the curve
Social distancing
Hand washing
Shelter in place
Self-isolation
Self-monitoring
Isolation
Drive through testing
Antiviral medicines

Personal protective equipment PPE
N 95 respirator
Ventilator
Vaccine
Mask
Social bubble

Heroes Forever

The quiet was deafening
I had walked into a COVID garden
The workers and gardeners were hollow inside
They were so focused on the horrors
They had never seen before
Life seemed without purpose
People struck down because of a hug or a kiss
With a beautiful person they loved

The virus claimed the rich and the poor
those left behind
Kings, presidents and rulers
So confused and disoriented
They looked to saving themselves and reputations
Before helping the many on ventilators

Nurses and doctors giving their lives
Holding the hands of precious souls
Who were starting their journeys to heaven
COVID was evil......But love would survive

The nurses and doctors
checkers and baggers at stores
Police and firemen
You helped us survive

Heroes you are
all in your own way
forever in our hearts
grateful for your aid

Jerry 2020

The Pandemic Changed our Lives

We use a telephone
To get food from restaurants

For church
We listen to a pod cast

We no longer sign
Credit card bills

We use zoom to talk with groups for
Business and friends

We wear the ubiquitous
mask everywhere

We no longer shake people's hands
Even after winning at sports

We social distance
and never hug
not even grandpa
The pandemic has changed our lives
But not our hearts

For we try to live fully
filling our thoughts with contentment
and dancing in the moment

Quarantine

It's like I said goodbye to
tomorrow
before it ever came

Yesterday
is in my diary but
it looks so much like the day before

I can't remember if it is
a Tuesday or a Wednesday

The future is like a foggy cloud
I remember my days
by the food I eat

Today I day a wore a mask
into the store

I felt like such a rebel
grabbing a package of cookies
on my way through the bakery

And now a precious small
gift of hope appears

you saying
We will meet again and
be able to hug
Someday soon

The Beautiful Old Inn at OV

The Inn at Ocean Village
where now no one goes
Because of Covid
once welcomed everyone

Thick old glass doors
creaking stairs
voices mingling from the bar
Greet each lucky guest

Wonderful old building smells
Mixed with those of delicious entrées
welcoming young ladies
warmly announcing
"Your reservation is ready "

Meeting friends at the bar
Was always a treat
friendly waitress who knew your name
Gin martini's (Tangueray for sure)
In iced glasses
Exquisite food served on
white table clothes eaten with
old friends and new
From around the nation

With music playing low and sweet

I breathe in the now
I want these moments to live on forever
My friend leans over and
says the words I wish to hear
Covid is done and over!
"Let me buy tonight!"

The Pandemic

The corona pandemic is
taking the joy out of
so much of our lives
When life is squeezed down
You need to look for the
little tidbits of joy
They remind us of the
happy future yet to come

Today I saw my first robin
Maple buds were covering
The top of my hot tub
Two birds just came to
My newly filled bird feeder
Neighbors on both sides have
Offered to get us anything we may need
We suggested toilet paper
They laughed and walked away!

Spring is coming!
The simple joys are now

The Year of COVID at our House

Refrigerator magnets now
hold up pictures and obituaries
of loved ones whom
COVID
has prematurely taken to heaven

Our morning coffee
And fire side conversation
Focuses on how our lives have changed

We talk about zoom meeting
have virtual doctor appointments

We hear about the loneliness of
our single friends who can't
see their grandchildren

Now we say we don't ever want to go to
a nursing home where
no one can visit you

But where should people go in
their twilight years

We ruminate how if we were young again
how different life would be

A first kiss carries so much more
Then when we were young
Is there such a thing as a virtual first kiss

So we read books
clean the house
straighten the garage
talk to our friends by phone
and watch the occasional
TV program

Waiting for this time
of Covid
to
End

In My Opinion
Chapter Five

Hurricane

We knew it was coming
weeks before it
became a household name

It was just a green dot on
the screen off in the
Atlantic Ocean where storms are born

Like unwanted birthdays or
a pending dentist appointment
We anticipated its arrival

One day the little dot got larger
Still moving slowly across the
great expanse of ocean

Initially not talking about it
then checking on it daily with growing concern
the weather channel had hourly reports on it

We casually checked our emergency supplies
we mentioned it in passing to those around us
it's approach began to bend our reality

Reviewing insurance policies
updating friendships with relatives and friends in
the north that have extra bedrooms

Filling gas cans, water bottles and extra pet food
It seemed there was nothing out there to stop its
relentless, violent, turbulent, pelting rain and wind
Progressing right towards the center of where we live

The closer its approach
the more it's mere existence controlled
our lives
our conversations
our facade of bravery

Remembering friends and others who
stayed through previous storm's

It's now a day away
And folks are praying
Even the atheists

Just Like You
(a deaf child)

I see the rising sun
Just like you
I feel the warmth of hugs
Just like you
I love watching bugs and
Chasing butterflies
Just like you

I eat tacos and
Moose tracks Ice cream
I savor it on my lips
just like you
From the way you smile and
Give me a thumbs up

It must be your favorite too

When the morning sun rises
Birds chirp and sing and
I see beautiful colors
Coming out of the birds
mouths
I enjoy playing outside
Just like you

The world is such a
wonderful place for me
And when you take
The time to talk to me
We both share the wonder of the world
And our lives in a special way
And you can see
I'm just like you!

gerald poet 6/18/2019

Mossy

I love moss

I could walk on it everyday
It Make my toes happy

It makes me feel like I'm walking
On a cloud
A green, moist, cool, cloud

I even wish I could
Floss with moss

Moss makes me think
I'm in a special place
Where leprechauns live
An there are small doors near the earth
To enter into big trees (where they have cookies!)

There are just so many relaxing
And beautiful things about moss
Yet some would rather have grass
Which seems rather selfish

Some folks think in Heaven streets are paved with gold
If I have a vote I'd vote for moss
Then we could all go bare foot all the time
I really do like moss!

A Poem Lives Forever

A poem lives forever
Revealing the
joys - love and hope of
Being

It discloses the roads we've traveled
To those who travel
Close or years behind

Poems follow us
Read or uttered
Beside smoldering Campfires
Roaring fire places
With red wine or
Delicious Coffee

They may become our
History and collected memories
Collectors

With rhyme and discriminating word
poetry touches our
core and emotion
It says we lived
our lives had meaning
and most of all
loved

God
Writes poetry
about spectacular
sunsets, sweet
newborn babies
and deeds well done

Poetry

The cadence and rhyme of iambic pentameter
Is at once familiar and comforting

The rhyme scheme and structure of a sonnet
Is dignified and classic

The structure of a villanelle
Is elaborate and grand

The unmetrical irregular flow of free verse
Is unrestrained and liberating

The compact brevity of haiku
Is both direct and elegant

The irreverence of a limerick
Is numerous and often naughty

The simplicity of a nursery rhyme
Is basic and reassuring

And all are the wonderful part of a language
That is poetry [Randy Flory] Ran

Politics and Weather

How can I hold
Friends and relatives
in contempt for
Their support of
rogues and dictators
And their often silly and destructive behaviors

Their views have
No historical or scientific basis
No religious basis
No constitutional accuracy
Not even common sense

When these close relatives say with pride
They have never read a book
Since high school
Never gone to college and
The entirety of the news they get
Is from a conspiracy channel
I am frustrated beyond belief

We were raised together
Celebrated life event's together
Now I when we meet
I find the only topics we can discuss
Are
Sports and the weather

Taking Today into Tomorrow

The beauty of today is
Often overshadowed by
My waking mood

Leaving bed grumpy
Unfinished chores
Laundry in multiple piles
Resolutions organized on yellow pads
I stumble confusingly into today

Then unexpectedly
A beautiful woodpecker
Knocks on my house
The coffee is just perfect
Enchanting smell, nice and hot
My spouse bought me Star Bucks !!!

I don't want to leave this morning!
The mail carrier walks to my door
A special delivery card is
placed in my hand
I don't read the address or name
I just see in large letters
I LOVE YOU NOW AND WILL FOR EVER!

I want to hold this moment
I embrace it
And take it with me into tomorrow
An all the future tomorrows

The Gift of a Word

A Jewish friend
Gave me a gift
I will enjoy forever

She said my poetry was "Hamish"
Which is Yiddish and means
Simple, homey and cozy

I was not familiar with the word
However its nuanced meaning
Expresses in a concise form
The ideas I'm often trying
To convey in my
Wandering use of words

For in poetry
The gift of a word
In a small and delicious way
Expands one's world

I remember when a high school teacher
Said I was erudite

Just learning that word motivated
Me to identify with it

The gift of a word....
I tell my grand children
"You are intelligent and resourceful"

Tips

I am trying to figure out
What denominations of US currency
Waiters and waitresses and
oil change employees like best

Silver and copper coins don't
Get so much as a smile
Dollar bills are okay but the
Receivers pocket them with
Hardly a nod

Fives seem to get a better response
Receivers are and happy and grin
10 dollar bills get their attention
"Have a good day!"

But the group-of receivers
who serve so faithfully and well
Love $20 bills the best
They know a mistake has not been made

People aren't foolish with $20 dollar bills
So when a twenty dollar tip
Is laid out
It's too big to refuse

They give thanks by flirting
(which is worth the tip right there)
Thank excessively and quietly think
“This is the most wonderful person
I’ve met today”

I love $20 dollar bills!

Tulips

The yellow tulips stood
So tall and stately on
The dinner table

Into this cold Michigan winter
They came - probably
From thousands of miles away

Across oceans wrapped tightly
In deep buckets of frigid ocean water
To the table in my home

I told them they warmed my spirits
To let me share the little
Space and time we had
Here on this earth together

Then they wilted and
Gently began to fall apart
And I tenderly placed each beautiful
Wilting petal in its final respite

They made the world a better more beautiful place
And when I travel to my resting place I hope the
Same will be said for me

Gerald poet 1/23/2022

Favorites from Sharing the Jerky
Chapter Six

How to Read Poetry

fishing is best done
with fishermen
Baseball best done
with a team
Thinking is best done
alone or
with engineers
Parties are more fun
with friends

But poetry is best written
alone
when beauty is all around
and best read by
candlelight
a glass of wine and
the beauty of your smile

together they make me feel like
Samuel Beckett or
William Shakespeare and
even Robert Frost

Bad Poetry

I like to write bad poetry
because
good poetry is hard to write
And
folks have such high expectations for it.

It's recited in
social circles of high regard
with such an air
by people who have pedigrees
and pompousness.

There are good things about words
poorly stated,
which don't rhyme
and look elementary.
It makes people feel superior,
they don't have to think too much,
they smile and grin when they read it,
no one worries about iambic pentameter
or whether its classic or new age.

Bad poetry lets me write about
dogs, trucks, trains, guns and bad behaviors.
I can use dangling participles and split Infinitives,
write thoughts and words common folk
understand and use to get through each and every day.

People of high society- blue bloods - would never venture to use or read this type of poetry.

Bad poetry can be cool
on the street or even in school.
So the question for you is -
do you like bad poetry?
or just Browning,
Frost and
Homer?
Are you enjoying this?
This is a sad, bad poem........
or maybe not ....

Snow

Little white crystals
fall and swirl
from the sky
into a dream world
where
fluffy white blankets
are
carefully being
laid over houses
cars
bird nests
and slow moving old men

A Conversation with God

The wind blows cold today
on the Appalachian Trail.
I eat oatmeal, drink my coffee,
and while lifting my pack I ask
"Please walk with me today God".

A friend would be nice today
in these strange woods with
mountains to climb.
What did you do yesterday God?
I hiked, rested and wrote a poem.

Did you visit India?
Do you know most Americans think You
live in the U.S. and just
visit other places?
Who would you visit if you weren't
with me today;
the president? famous people? a guy in prison?

Of all the places in the world,
why are you walking here with me?
Want to race to that big tree up ahead?
Tell me if I'm not being respectful enough.
Should I be dressed up to be talking with you?
When I eat jerky can you taste it too?

Why do I find you in the woods
more often than in church?
Have you ever talked to Socrates?

Was he as bright as folks think he was?

How is it that I know you are walking
with me and yet hear no footsteps?
Is it true that you spend more time
with those who read holy books?

This GORP is tasty,
God, want some?

Limping into the Wilderness

I should have gone into the
wilderness years ago
in my prime
with defined guns which
made the local beauties gasp
when the pool, in frothy splashes, took in my ripped
svelte and toned body.

But today with greying hair,
pill bottles bulging, cell phone, weakening resolve
and lighter necessities only pack
I limp into the wilderness.

Only a day or two
to find nature
but most of all to prove
I'm an adventurer, a wilderness guy,
a red-blooded man in every sense
(and a poet?)
the kind of gent
who makes even
older girls and sophisticated ladies
well past their prime,
think thoughts of
cowboys, pirates, explorers,
adventurers, Marco polo
and ME!

You Are Here

I keep thoughts of
your smile
in the top of my pack
and echoes of
your laughter
strewn through my things.

I watch reflections of
your eyes
in the morning dew
and smell
your perfume
in the flowers and trees.

As I walk down the trail
and
climb the mountains
I talk to you
softly
and hear you in the breeze.

I see you walking
in the shadows
asking me
to
dance with you
in
the clouds.

Campground Fly

Ah, my life as a fly.
Sometimes we travel
in circles supreme.
Sometimes we land on a dog
or get stuck on a cake.

Today I'm stuck in a john
down under the seat.
The views are terrible at best,
for no one likes big butts
and little butts too,
all with something to say.

They blot out the light
and rumble and cuss
and there are hazards galore.
For some only an umbrella is
necessary, but

Bombs are the worst,
for hissing and swirling they come,
and cause such a splash.

A poor friend named Herman
is still riding a wave
that started in February
and ended in May!

Campground Mosquito

As campground mosquitos
our rules are all set.
When SUV doors open with
joy and glee
we're organized,
attack plans in place
formations all set.

As pop tops go up
we zoom and we buzz
and gather donations
that put the
Red Cross to shame.

City folk give the most
all plump and fat
but seldom can smack us
as we dive by.

Then in the night
when sunburned and red
they donate some more
to the little Red Cross volunteers
always asking for more!

My Old Tent

It's old and gray
and beginning to fray
it weighs too much
smells like burning weeds
and oh the fuss to set it up.

new tents are way cool
so easy to go up
they're bright in color
have great modern design
which make them best

yet my tent is like an old friend
with rips and tears
smells and dried bug remains
it brings back memories of
adventure and
excitement from the past

it has never let me down
so it goes with me each summer
smell, rips, tears, bugs, and all
and like a good friend
it will go with me on new adventures
down the trail

Whisper Your Name

When I am away
in the dark of the night
I whisper your name

I think of your beauty
the sparkle of your eyes
in the rain
I whisper your name

I feel your presence
see your smile in my thoughts
in the shadows
I whisper your name

I see you in fluffy clouds
asking me to sit
in the bright sun with you
I whisper your name

and wait
for you
to whisper back
to me

Why Give Your Love Flowers

Love must be celebrated,
respected and cherished
to keep it strong
and make it grow.

Without attention
it sputters and loses its spirit
like a starving fire
on a rain-soaked day.

There are many
gifts and actions that make love
grow and sparkle.
Romantic gifts seem best,
chocolate, jewelry, music,
dancing in the rain
and homemade pies

Flowers are my
gift of choice.
They are special
as if God just made them for a
beautiful lover.
Their exploding colors,
fragrant smells,
intrinsic beauty.
fragile short life

tell the world that you
are in love.

They are to enjoy
in the moment
in the now.
Giving them is a special,
universal moment
for lover and loved

Life is like the flower,
beautiful,
short lived,
to be enjoyed in the moment
and celebrated
hopefully with
a kiss or two!

It's Cold Here Tonight

It's cold
without your love
here with me
When you
are not here
I need
a sweater
Turn up the heat
Drink warm liquids
Sit in the sun
Stay in bed longer
It's no use,
I just get chilled
Return to me
Be near
and warm
my soul.

When You Were There

When life is done
and
I look back
the days were best
when
you were there

The simple joys
became a feast
my load was
lighter
the days
brighter
when
you were there

Grandpa's Wilderness Camping Rules

Parents have rules
Teachers have rules
The Bible has rules
Even condos have rules
But Grandpa's camping rules are different
And maybe even strange
No singing "Grandma got run over by a reindeer"
No monkey business
No funny business
No skunk business
(I'm not even sure what a business is!)

Food must be cooked over a smoky fire
Hot dogs must be slightly burned
Beans must be eaten with a
bent plastic spoon
Scary stories must be told every night
about bears and wolves chasing
kids bringing fresh baked bread
to a starving grandma who lives
in a faraway woods
(don't all grandmas live in
old age homes in the city?)

I guess I can put up with these rules
Cause some of the rules I actually enjoy
Like Ice cream cones for breakfast
No combing your hair if you don't want to

Wearing the same clothes all week
Not having to stay clean

But best of all
If you don't understand the rules
Or break them accidentally
You can get extra hugs and
maybe even Extra ice cream by
pretending you are A tiny bit scared
Of this wilderness living !

Grandmother's Dishes

(garage sale time)

Faded cracked and yellow
soup bowls missing
gravy urn still shiny and bright
gold rim on plates
looking brownish red

They sit
stacked beside
old novels
and fiction
well past today's interest

Waiting to be sold
at prices discounted
many times over

The joy
and celebrations
they saw
still lingers
reflected

in the memories
of aged buyers passing by

Christmas parties
graduations
birthdays
anniversaries
They were featured at all

Piled high with
pork roast
mashed potatoes
vegetables
and cakes
of all colors and styles

Handled so lovingly
dried only by hand
placed carefully
in China cabinets so fine
out of reach of
sticky, dirty, little hands

Awaiting a future they
hope will once again be
filled with
good food and
happy families.
To hear
Silent Night
and Happy Birthday
sung out of tune -

at least one more time

Cats

cats are cool
they do what they want
and say what they please
sleep on chairs
or place themselves
on your lap
without ever asking

we serve them
food
and take out
their poop
we comb their fur
and scratch
their heads
and let them
sleep on our beds

cats live such
good lives
most would say

wherever
cats go when
they die is
where I hope
I shall
one day lie

Losing Weight

This morning
I thought about losing weight
just ten pounds or so
Exciting thin thoughts
raced through my mind

Could I handle the compliments?
"damn you look good "
"so young I didn't recognize you "
"college reunion this summer? "

A reason to get new clothes

Might have to change my Facebook page

A few dance lessons
would go nicely with my new figure

A crash course in dealing
with friends' jealousy wouldn't hurt
even if it's an on line course

What about a new sport for me?
I love watching
Olympic gymnasts and
beach volley ball

And so with bathrobe flapping and
South Beach,
Weight-Watchers and
grapefruit diets
flooding my mind

I head toward the fridge

To get this thing on the road
a V8 and hard-boiled egg

Opening the fridge
the light created a halo around
last nights double cheese,
deep dish
extra pepperoni pizza
~
It was delicious

Squirting the Stars

With squirt gun loaded she says,
"Let's squirt the stars, Grandpa."
That will make the night dark,
I tell the little blond girl.
Let's just squirt the moon.
We squirted low to miss the stars
and got the moon!!
It started to fade.
"What will the cow jump over"
she squealed in delight?
The man in the moon has
dealt with little squirts before!
Most squirts never get there.
It's usually as dry as a sandbox,
but if you sing "hay diddle diddle,
the cat and his fiddle
the cow jumped over the moon"
and have a little laughing dog on your lap
and are careful with grandma's plates
A spoon may go dashing by......
"How does the silverware
get out of the drawer?"

I don't know,
but getting the moon wet with squirt guns
Is a sure way to give the man living there chills.
Little blond girls with squirt guns
can be so dangerous!!!

Shower Patina

men must have a dominate gene
a "patina attractor device"
for antiques
well-aged artifacts
things that are rusty,
musty and dusty

not only do they seem to
enjoy flee markets
old tractors
and trains
whenever they rinse
they create
"shower patina"

in the showers and tubs that they use
the browns and the golds
that forms on the sides
growing and glowing
with each passing day
all soapy and clingy
a site to behold

now ladies
of distinction and class
find this demeanor
disgusting and crass
a health factor

for sure
to be remedied
with powerful sprays
and long handled brushes

lest mother in law
in shower
should happen to fall
and end up cussing them all !

Athletes Beware

Injuries lurk everywhere
when seniors play sports
Love the tennis but
tennis elbow waits to come courting and
planter aphasia wants to be your doubles partner
While aching Achilles tendon
rotator cuff and Mr Hamstring
All want matches......
Golf is a delight
Fresh air with friends
a few swings and then
Oh! my back!
And what about getting the
clubs out of the car!
Ouch!
Pickle ball scores
such a strain on the brain
we aging folks are slipping
Alzheimer's - dementia can't be far behind
Shuffleboard dangers are lurking with
biscuit cuts and tang contusions
Fishing sounds great
but hooks and barbs all sharp and pointy
just waiting to catch you
in inappropriate places
Bike riding is always a breeze
until vertigo spins the world
like a carousel gone wild

With injuries ready to pounce
it is hard to leave the
safety of condo and house

But onward we push
for athletes we are
Forget injuries and pain
Chiropractor
Doctors and
dentists
are awaiting our call
Round robin @ 8:00
Golf @ 11:00
Bocci @ 2:00
Pickle @ 3:00
Shuffleboard @ 5:00
Happy hour @ 6:00
Dinner @ 7:00
Bridge @ 8:00
Do these seniors ever take naps?

Do Feet Get Enough Credit

(the agony of de-feet)

My name is Feet and
today I am
hurting and tired
And why shouldn't I?
I carried "team body" all day
yet everyone looks down on me
The right arm swung the racket for
two hours and then it could rest
Face smiled several times
But I had to carry it all day
Stomach may be the worst offender of everyone
It loads up on
pizza, beer and ice cream
then I have to carry the whole load
Even the skin misuses me
If it feels cool
Coats, hats, gloves and more go on
I carry all that stuff over ice and snow
And as a group
They make me do my work
In smelly dirty socks and too small shoes
If I complain about a little pain
They call me names
Like "hammer toe" or "bunion foot"
Or even "athletes foot"
Which sounds ok but really is a
Put-down that nobody wants

Sometimes the crowd up there
Misses and we even get sprinkled on
So what are we to do?
It seems we do all the work without much credit
So if you are ever hanging out with the crowd upstairs
How about just saying once
"my you have beautiful feet"

Senior Bicycles

Like tombstones in a cemetery
well past their prime
with leaning
faded markers
they stand In disciplined racks.
Row upon row
most rusted, dented and busted
old squeeze horns on handlebars askew
with tires so narrow
they look like an arrow.
Wide white wall tires
once in the trend
now flat and cracked
like the surface on the moon.
Fluttering ripped plastic bags cover
huge broad seats large as a Webber
baskets of wicker, plastic and canvas
2" x 4" trailer hitches
for golf carts, shopping carts and more.

Colors once bright
which use to
delight youngsters
who thrilled to their ride
now chipped and faded
grays and light browns.

These valiant
old models
squeak and groan when rode
Some with padlocks
to protect from thieves
who never come
Yet like their riders
often will give more
good years
of wonder and joy
to all who their use
want to employ
(ever wonder why seniors seldom buy new bicycles?)

A Book

I look
upon a book
and often see
stories told of
maidens, men
or philosophy

of horses
dogs
mysteries and
things yet
untold

I love my books for
they will be
with me and
keep me company
when
I shall walk into
my last night
and death
shall be my mate

they will give me
hope and
joy
for books like
beer, wine

and good friends are
easy company

More Quirky Jerky!
Chapter Seven

Condo Rules

CLOSE THE GARAGE DOORS
NO CLOTHES LINES
EACH UNIT WILL BE PAINTED THE SAME COLOR
NO FLAGS OUT FRONT
QUIET PLEASE
NO PETS ALLOWED
NO ROLLER BLADING
SKATEBOARDING NEVER
LAWNS CUT TO 1"
NO KITE FLYING ALLOWED
DO NOT PARK TRAILERS OUT FRONT
NO CHILDREN UNDER 50 PLEASE
TURN RADIOS DOWN
NO LATE NIGHT PARTIES
NO FLOWERPOTS ON DECKS
DO NOT WASH CARS IN DRIVEWAYS
NO OVERNIGHT GUESTS
DO NOT FEED THE BIRDS
ALL CARS PARKED IN THE GARAGE AT NIGHT
NO CAR ON STREET AFTER 10:00 PM
NO SOLICITING
NO COOKIE SALES - THIS MEANS GIRLS SCOUTS TOO
NO TRICK OR TREATING
NO GARAGE SALES
NO RUNNING ON THE SIDEWALKS
NO CHRISTMAS LIGHTS OUT FRONT
(YOU MAY PUT OUT WHITE 6" CANDLE
IN CENTER OF LIVING ROOM WINDOW ONLY)
APPROVED CONDO GREETING
"ANOTHER WONDERFUL IN PARADISE"

Mr. Stiff and Achy

A new friend lives at our house.
He slipped in
when we weren’t looking.
He's not loud or noisy,
but he's such a pain.

He's at our back
when we pick up things,
climb the stairs,
or make the bed.

He's right there
every morning
when we get out of bed.
He's even in the shower
when we drop the soap.

But now
he has a name
"Mr. Stiff-n-achy"
and
I think I like him more.

He says he is going to live here
for lots of years to come.

At least
he is easier to complain about
than the cats
or my wife.

My Glasses

They are on
my head
until I'm dead.
They go with me
in rain
and snow.

They are
by my bed
each night
when I lay me
down to sleep.

They sparkle
when they are clean.
Some say
they make
me look intelligent.

They help me see
and hold
my nose in place.

I love
my glasses
for when I die
and turn to dust
my glasses

will be
all that is
left of me.

The City Camp

(at Traverse City State Campground)

the throbbing roar
Of the Harleys
ate the morning's
silence
too quickly
to enjoy any
lingering
dreams

faint night
memories of
coolers being
sacked
by hungry coons
disappear
in the calls
of gulls
scrapping
over refuse
left by last nights
sleeping campers

Games Can Hear the Rain

They hear
the pitter patter
of the
rain
and see
the drops
streaking windowpanes

It is then
the games get
bold
and quickly unfold as
they come from under beds
and push open
seldom used cupboards

They squiggle from behind
chests of drawers
jump up on tables
or just sprawl on the
floor

Their pieces and dice
spread out in attack
causing players
to yell
and occasionally show
strife

But when the sun
shows through the windows
and falls onto the floor
They head for
cupboards
slide under the beds
waiting for
rain
fog
or even some snow

New Car Meets Trade-In

They sit side by side
briefly
on the new car lot
flags flying.

Smiling, plaid jacketed
sales staff
greeting customers
like oldest of friends.

Only a short
glance of introduction
between the two.

The new
shiny and bright
brisling with electronic
gadgets and gizmos
eager to take on tomorrow.

The old
tired and bent
smelling of French fries,
baby vomit,
and spilled coffee,
tires dirty and wore,
paint faded and splotchy,

dents from Frisbee, baseball
and hail.

The new
proud
of the high price it demands.

The old
embarrassed
by the pittance offered in return.

After all the trips to the store
school, hospital and even the time
we pulled mother in law
out of the ditch,

would just $50 more
be asking too much?

Our Car's Interior

(tell who we are)
With bobble heads,
hanging dice,
and ten-year-old ash trays
half filled with coins
some cars are like
riding in a Family Dollar Store.
Religious cars
have crosses hanging
on mirrors,
St. Christopher praying
on the dash,
and baby Jesus riding
shotgun in the back window.
Pet lover's cars
smell like dogs,
have Kibble and Bits
on the floor,
chewed throw toys under the seats
and half-filled water dishes
which splash on your shoes.
Fast food lovers
have cars that
smell like French fries
are filled with McDonald bags
and cups with
every available door pocket

filled with
catchup, mustard and
leaking mayonnaise containers.
New parent's cars
are fitted with car seats,
twisted mirrors
to watch every little smile and toot
hanging toys to entertain,
blankets, books, and diapers,
and the ubiquitous "Baby on Board" sign.
OCD cars are unbelievably neat,
pine tree air fresheners hanging,
leather so clean it squeaks,
map stored neatly in the back seat pocket,
windows sparkle brightly
(no finger prints on these)
even the keys shine
The eclectic hoarders is my favorite of all.
You can find coupons for
anything on the floor,
old condiment packets on the seats,
church bulletins from Christmas 2010
library books,

numerous cassettes with
tape hanging out,
toys, empty cans, clothes,
perhaps
your missing sweatshirt
from the family reunion
three years ago.

It labors climbing hills
with its cargo in tow,
but it's home on the go -
even if there is an over riding
feeling that you are traveling
in a dumpster on wheels!

Little Lights

I love little lights
on Christmas trees
candles in windows
flashlights in pup tents
soft lights in church
and twinkling stars.
Sitting close to
small campfires
reading books under blankets
dim lights in halls.
Little lights
with glow so small
say come be with me
my spirit is yours
to nourish and hold.

I find God in little lights
It seems He
needs me to
love and share the
warmth in
even the littlest of
lights.

Morning Coffee

It is hot
It is brown
I love its taste and
of all the food I know
it gives the greatest comfort

It greets me every day
with smells so fine
It is there
when days are hot
and surely there
when days are cold

It's been with me
watching children grow
and on the trail
after funerals it is there
even to church
it sometimes goes

it is drunk with friends
relatives
in-laws and outlaws
I've drunk it from plastic
paper, tin and glass
beer mugs
wine glasses
and sippy cups

it's best
when I'm alone
for it helps
me think of you
with
cat on lap
slippers and housecoat

Willie's Last Day of School

Willie
was very poor
just up from Mississippi
sat near the back
his eyes seldom moved
his mouth never

Did Willie have dreams
hopes,
ambitions to be great
or successful?

Had he ever loved someone?
Did someone love him?
What was his favorite song?
Did he ever have a pet?
Had he ever seen Lake Michigan?
Did he have a brother?

The talkative, aggressive students
seemed to take all my time

Willie left today

My chance to know Willie is
gone
forever

6-1981
Ottawa High School

The Things That I Buy

the things I buy
I think
I need
I've told myself
and planned ahead
so when I get
just what I want
how happy I will be.

so now I have
the things I want
and knew I
needed,
but
as they age
and old they grow
I see them less
and less
and wonder

just
what it was that

made me think they were
the things I wanted
and thought I needed

I Am Running

I'm running
across the room
to get to grandma
down the halls
to get to class
through the aisles
to get the best sales
running
running
running
down the highway
to get to work
through the winter
to get to summer
through life's work
to get to retirement

but today I will walk
to hear grandma's
cricket story
to watch
the birds playing

to see
the flowers blooming
to smell
the cookies baking

to get
a hug from grandpa

runners often leave the present
too fast
to get to the future

The People That We Meet

The people that we meet
are peep holes
into the soul
of
the universe

The way we see them
and treat them
open
or closes
passageways into
the origins of
our beginnings

Together they form
a mosaic
which tells a story
of life's
origin
A history of the universe

People are the cells
that make up
the living hope
love and
All that many call
God

We are all part of its
magic wonder
Together we find
purpose and joy
and reason for
life itself

Life

milk
bicycles
first kisses
introspection
finding direction
education
choices
opportunities
options
transcending my constrictions
need to wander
new experiences
old friends
new friends
childhood myths
general relativity
quantum mechanics
donuts
coffeecake
love
ashes

Living in the Now

caught between
yesterday and tomorrow
like peanut butter and jelly
on a sandwich
we try to live fully in today
but feel the aches
and pains of yesterday
the anxiety
of what is coming tomorrow

hoping the doubts
cares and fears of today
will not appear in new shapes
and forms in the future

living in the now is our quest
fully, exciting, productive
being satisfied with hope
and simple joys
giving to those in need
getting rid of greed

we start by being calm
asking questions
taking suggestions from lives
well lived
taking small steps of kindness
and gratitude

helping the fallen
protecting the weak

like an infant we grow fast in wisdom
and knowledge
the now begins to feel comfortable
affordable, achievable, predictable
like the song of a bird
or a baby's first words

we feel the now
as we become more
and more
a part of the whole

Owning Stuff

When I was young
and times were tough
I'd seldom share
I loved my things
and giving stuff was very rough
for having things
and owning stuff
was such a joy
It made me feel such sweet success
the more I had
the more I stored
my basement overflowing

But now I'm old
and wiser some
and storing stuff
and owning things
is really quite a chore
Taking care of things
is just a bore
and moving things
is worst of all

Now I find sharing things
and giving stuff
has become my joy
This thing I give you now
is gone from me

and yet it's memory
gives me joy
would you like
some more stuff?

War

scares birds
mothers hate it
young people fight it
nations fear it
religion exacerbates it
songs glorify it
politicians exploit it
military plan it
citizens die in it
blood banks store for it
wives cry and grieve during it
soldiers are maimed in it
angels collect souls during it
gun factory's make money from it
the environment is destroyed from it
veterans remember it
children suffer from it
pacifists try to stop it
evil thrives during it
God allows it
poets write about it

love prevents it

More Favorites from Less Again!

Chapter Eight

More From Less

It seems impossible to
Get more from less

However we get more years to live
By eating less
We climb higher mountains with
Less weight in our packs

Our skin is more beautiful with
Less exposure to sun
We get more miles per gallon with
Less weight in the car

There is more closet space with
Less clothes on the racks
There are more complements with
Less pounds on our frame

Why then are so many of us
Attracted to more?

It could be because more is usually
Greater > than less
However, in many things like
Seeing a doctor
Paying taxes or
Gaining weight

Less is always best!
Just one more thing to think about.

The Elegance of Simplicity

There is something beautifully elegant
about simplicity and minimalism

The bounty of Thanksgiving dinner
can overwhelm the senses
however a meal of bread, cheese and wine
(preferably Kendall Jackson Chardonnay)
seems to focus the senses

A party of ten demands
a high degree of social acumen
and the conversational "noise"
may dim intellectual intercourse
Dinner with a few allows
participants to explore even the
smallest of ideas

The complexity of an airline cockpit confuses most
but the sleek simplicity of an Apple I-phone
can appeal to children
and yet they perform some of the same functions

Having much and storing collections
of stuff we do not need
wastes limited world resources and
personal energy
Using less conserves
so others may live more fully

Reading and writing fiction and
prose demand time and effort
Reading poetry is a fast
and easy way to one's emotions

Minimum word usage is
wonderful in its simplicity
It allows opportunities for elegance

Simplicity gives us more from less!

My Carbon Footprint

My lawn is brown, but
do I really need a green lawn?
I own a home so
do I need a summer home?

Shall I heat my cabin in the winter
when I'm not living there?
I have two cars
shall I buy another for my child?

What temperature
shall I keep my hot tub?
My house is 2,000 square feet
do I really need 1000 more
to match my neighbors?

Are these things so wrong?
I have worked hard
I should be able to get what I want

Should I vote for candidates
who want to protect the environment
or those who want to drill in the Arctic?
paper or plastic
the questions just keep coming

Do I need a car with 300 horsepower?
What about snow mobiles, speed boats
and motor bikes?

will there be any in Heaven

I don’t recall reading about “a carbon footprint”
in the Bible and my
clergyman doesn't talk about one

Maybe my carbon footprint
is just like global warming
something the experts talk about
but really doesn't affect me

Where Are You Going with the Hurry

You rushed to get to dinners end
covered the dishes
cleared the vegetables and salad

The wine was corked before
the second glass
all before I was done eating my first helping!
Why the hurry?

A slow glass of wine is so
enjoyable when had with friends
and yet the hurry

I struggled to eat my corn while
you were preparing dessert

Why the hurry?
Is something happening I should
know about?

You were putting away dishes
when all we wanted to do
was talk to you

Did you notice that
socialization is not possible
when you are in a
hurry to wash the dishes?

For just one meal
live in the now

lay your fork down between bites
push the hurry aside

tomorrow when I am gone
you can let the hurry return

Cats and Saints

Hello, Mr. Cat
You are sitting in my front yard again
I enjoy talking to you
You greet me every day
and I love that!

Did you know two popes became saints today?
Would you like to become a cat saint?
Do you think that's possible?

This thing about saints -
Do you think I
could become a saint?

I haven't been to Rome
I can't identify any of
the great art works
and
I'm not Polish or Italian

What if everyday
people could become saints
I'm a carpenter,
that should give me a head start

I would seriously like to
choose the next saint

It probably wouldn't be you Mr. Cat
but you could be best friend
to a saint!
I know several people
I think should be saints
They strive to do good every day
They help the poor,
give to the needy

They probably wouldn't
make sainthood

because they think
women are equal with men,
should be able to vote for popes
and think gays can marry

This saint stuff is so
hard to understand
Mr. Cat

I'm just glad you are here every day
to talk to
Thanks for being my friend
You are a good listener.

Enjoy your day, Mr. Cat.

Loaded Plates

I love the expression
"Everyone has so much on their plate"
I see a visual of a plate
with loads of life's stuff on it

Campers, cruises, and cottages
Bible studies and golf outings
financial managers and under takers
friends and relatives
stacked high
hanging over the sides
all on one
big
plate

Why do we load our plates so full?

We want to help
A needy mother-in-law
(dressed impeccably)who
needs a ride to visit out of town
grandkids
whose only ride is with us
when we want a romantic
weekend alone

We add pets to our busy lives
And become folks traveling
who now can only
stay at motels
that accommodate dogs
because "Prissy"
Our Chihuahua
with an attitude
needs socialization with other dogs

We volunteer to babysit
A grandson who
Is so active
he jumps off the loaded plate
to lock us out of
the bathroom
when you really have to go!

We buy
so many residences
we have to cancel
dinner reservations
to cut yards of the yards we own
We can only live in one at a time!

All on our plate

This loaded plate thing is a hoot
Maybe our plates
aren't too full
it's just that we have loaded
our plates with weird stuff.

Stuff that really
isn't that important
and the really important thing is the plate

Instead of putting more on
our plates
let's take one item at a time off
and either give it away
or put it in your best friends
to go box

Maybe they have
more room on their plate!

Someday an undertaker
will clear our plate
wash it
and give it to our kids

Maybe
It's not what we have
on our plate that counts
but what we have in our heart

Don't get me started!
Cholesterol, a-fib, pacemakers ....

Let's just read a poem!

Landline Phones

Seniors are often slow to drop landlines
just why is hard to say
they argue their merit with
determined angst
and righteous indignation

they remember their first date using
one and worry birds would not have
a place to sit without lines to sit on
to never see muscular repair men
climbing poles would just seen wrong

the familiar rings might mean
a gossipy new story was in the making
the whole house is wired for them
even the garage and laundry room
and the cost, the cost!!
kids have no idea

young folks think phones without apps
are like black and white TVs
typewriters, record players
and refrigerators without ice makers
anachronisms their aging parents talk about
but they have never seen

with seniors it might something more
maybe they just want the
world to slowdown
they are finally getting used
to touch tones and eight tracts!
now a new device comes along that is
hard to read and kids love them

something must be wrong or
sinful with the device
caring a phone with a camera
in your pocket - what might it see
down there?

having to learn new vocabulary
like apps, texting, social media and gigabyte
is just too much

and yes, seniors especially
don't like the name "cell" phone!

A Cup of Coffee

I bought my friend
A cup of coffee today
Didn't think to much about it
Just a cup of black coffee

Was it a wasted expense
A reckless foolish act
Or did this little deed
Plant a small and precious seed

Will I be here a year from now
To buy another tasty cup
Will we be here together
To enjoy another special brew

Will you or I
be able to remember
The beanie bitter taste
The friendship that we shared over
each and every steaming cup

I bought a cup of coffee today
Because you and your smile
are here with me today

And every chance I get to buy
A hot and steaming cup
Says to me

Today is a treasure
And I'm glad to share it
With you....

Frogs

Have you ever wondered
What frogs think about?

If they live near a golf course
It's probably getting hit by golf balls

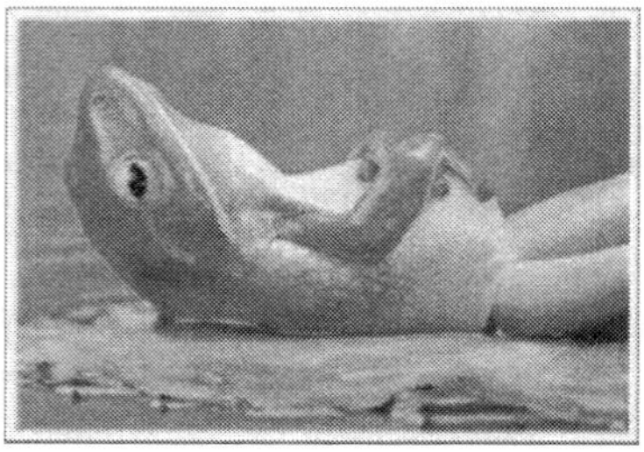

Those that dwell in ponds worry
about getting poked by little
boys with sticks

Some may just think
about bugs and flies

A few could be concerned that
their friends have
longer tongues than theirs

Pondering how far they could jump
would be an interest

Or conclusions
maybe they
Jump to conclusions
But I think they mainly think
about croaking

They seem to want
the whole world
to know when they croak!

My Epitaph

The last big thing
for family and friends
will be to write an epithet
for me on a stone
however small

I could write it now
but I'm sure the words
would please mainly me

Family would probably prefer
short epithets
that are less pricy and
to the point

"cranky in life
even with a beautiful wife"

Would they use stickers
if they could?
maybe burn letter into
a crude wooden cross?

They might want conspicuous words
for all to see

"He rests in peace"
"In heaven he is well liked"

“Restless on earth, content in the afterlife”

But I think if simple words are best
and cost a factor too
just pen these words for
all to see

"He helped the needy"

The Goofy Googly-Ness of Life

For some people life is a puzzle
for others life is to be lived
straight as an arrow in
dresses and ties

For my grandchild and me,
we wish to live it
goofy and googly

practicing upside down smiles
reading books backwards
counting lighting bugs
In jars
eating ice cream pies for breakfast
talking to make believe friends
creating bazaar inventions
and taking the time
to be best friends

So when life gets heavy
resort to the goofy
Googly-ness of life!

A Paper Towel Poem

(when a poem was written on a paper towel)

I hung in the public restroom
three days
waiting to be used
listening to noises
and sounds
that would make a
lumberman blush

I just knew in the end
I would be rolled up,
wet, crushed into a ball
and thrown in the trash

used, abused,
and maybe misguided
upon the floor

But now I find myself under
pen and quill
of a paperless poet waiting
for his wife

rhyming words of thought and
joy printed on my face

which goes to prove
even bathroom paper

towels can become
special pages in life's
surprising story!

Campground Bears

camping just would not be as stimulating
or exciting without
stories shared
experiences recounted
and facts explained
about bears
usually black
sometimes brown
but
grizzly is best

information's given on
very dark nights to
new campers and
kids around flickering
sputtering campfires

every well-traveled camper
has a tale about an
800-pound bear
in the campsite
on a moonless night
stealing food and
causing trouble
while
campers were nervously in
tents looking for their flashlights
(with dead batteries)

or confronting one on the trail
when others in the group
were far, far ahead
too far to hear you yell

If the storyteller didn't see
or experience a real bear
they at least listened to
stores from long ago
of children walking miles to school
and seeing bears which
made their hair stand on end
and gave them fear of
bears for life

all the bears were very large
vicious and ready to attack
usually when the person
was alone and unprotected

it only makes sense then
by one who has experienced
far too many bears
(hence the gray hair)
that I should come up with a
few practical suggestions
for avoiding bear
encounters

Angie's Tooth Fairy

Tooth-fairies are special
to little girls and boys

Angie's tooth fairy had
some special magical powers
just for her

When the house is locked up
and all windows closed
her personal fairy enters
right through the glass window

Girls have girl fairies
and boys have boy fairies
(I suppose that's all
about that privacy thing
little girls are learning about)

Most kids get nickels and dimes but
Angie got a silver dollar not
because of inflation, but because
she is so special

Her grandpa told her that he
had heard long ago in a far away land
a difficult child had received
a handful of stones

It's a bit difficult to believe such a
grandpa story but it makes the
silver dollar fairy all the more special
Grandpa also says that tooth-fairies
can only bring coins through
solid glass windows and
definitely not stones

something about it being "too much of a pane"

I'm Stuck in a Poem

I'm stuck in
a poem and can't
get out

I tried a rhyme
or two
but they sounded flat

I repeated phrases
but they were
echoed word mazes

I used Alliteration
but the
words became
dissident

Will I wander about
In this poem forever
bumping into phrases
Stumbling over words?

Living in an ode
may not be so bad
for if this
becomes my abode
I'll for ever
live in a poem

When you read it
you may think
Jerry is stuck
in a very bad poem
and give
me a word of advice

It may be
just what I need
to get me out
and find a
a less wordy home

Grandma's Wish

Grandma served me some sauerkraut
I must not pout
and cannot shout
I know what's this is all about

served in a pretty dish
I know it is her tiny wish
that just like fish
I'll think its delish

This stuff that looks like cabbage fingers
With a taste that forever lingers

She hopes with just one bite
I'll get over my fright
And eat what's right

And maybe even learn to eat

Brussels sprouts!!

It's Tough Being an iPad

Have you ever thought
what it would be like
to be an iPad
for just one day?

People would poke
and touch you all
day long - Yuk!

They'd slide their fingers
across your screen
smearing your glass
yell at you for mistakes they've made

children fight over you
jabbing at you instead of
"touching" you

music is on continually
games are played for hours
the weather is checked repeatedly

the news is read and reread
from a variety of sources
(Do they think the news will change?)

You look for and
deliver e-mail
from all over the world!
then have to respond to said messages
And when you feel weak and
run down, someone
sticks a plug in you
(I'm not even going to say where!)
to give you an electrical charge

So my friend don't be sad
you are not an iPad
Be glad it's YOU doing the
poking,
touching.
swiping,
yelling,
playing,
looking,
reading
writing
and
charging!

Today's Power Lunch

I had lunch with my 7 year old
Granddaughter today

Power lunches seldom
Begin like today's
with
My guest holding my hand
From the car to the restaurant

It was refreshing
I should try it
with other clients

Chocolate milk and pizza
Is not the usual fare for
Normal power lunch partners

But when she offered me a drink of her milk
And slice of her pizza
I thought this lady
Knows how to get to business fast

Conversation was light
And focused on holiday giving
She asked about my wife
I found her polished and adorable

She starting talking about Ivy League Collages!
It was then I asked for the check.

How to Bore Friends

I have thought a lot about
how to bore my
aging sophisticated friends
who, like me, seem to have
time to give to this important
activity of personal affirmation

We are most likely to go down
this path when
reacquainting with old friends

First by promoting
pompousness and self accomplishments
as if they were constructive progress
on the social class scale

So how do we bore our friends ?

recounting personal health problems
is almost always tops and
sharing our friend's tragedies and
life threatening illnesses

Grand kids superior
intelligence is a given
and their athletic prowess
is our genetic gift to them

The cost of personal prescriptions
rates high on the list and
everyone always has the
"Best doctors" in the state

Recent travels to jungles and
cruises to places with strange
sounding names will have listeners
looking at iPhones for games to play
Of course
recent dinning experiences'
the lowest gas prices
(Which we seem to have just missed)
the importance of land lines and
defending yesterday's technology

I must not forget
coupon successes or
"shared time condo" experiences
purchased at half price

But boredom
is temporary and our friendships
are thinning
so with determined resolve
we ask,

"What did you have for lunch in Uruguay's ghettos?"
"Your friend John just seems too young for dementia!"
"Yes, little Jimmy sure is a great hopscotch player."

And so to move for a change

I ask " Have you seen any good movies lately ?"
Or "How did you ever snag two
for one coupons for Fred's
on a Tuesday night?!!"

Thin Wins

big and broad
most would applaud
super-sized
is the most prized
large mouthed
double decked
extra value
two for one
all draw us in

but for me
thin is in
and will always win

thin mints
wheat thins
thin sliced ham

I enjoy reading a thin book
and dating thin girls

however some large things
do get my attention
A fat billfold
A huge slice of apple pie a la mode
And a big kiss from my sweetie!

Summer's End

cottages looking forlorn and closed
screen doors no longer banging
the squeals and laughter of
carefree children now just fading echoes

beaches are empty and wind swept
porch furniture covered and tipped
ready to shed rain and snow

boats pulled far up onto land
those without sails sit
huddled near the trees
discussing which was the swiftest

fishing poles hang on walls
some with hooks, dried bait still attached
others with bobbers hanging limp

flag poles without ole' glory
point upward to pale blue skies
summer has ended at the lake

flower gardens overgrown
a few gold and yellow mums
peering out from rows of
rotting tomatoes still on the vine

corn stalks brown with age
misshaped pumpkins
awaiting Halloween

summer has ended in the garden

camping gear stored on shelves
plastic pools put in storage
bicycles collecting dust
garden tools dull and
still muddy and dirty
awaiting a good washing before
they are stored for the winter
summer has ended in the garage

meals of chili and soup replace
fruit and popsicle treats
photos of summer trips and
youth camps are
looked at one more time before
they are placed lovingly in albums

no one has to announce it when
the big yellow "limo"
stops out front in the morning

everyone knows

SUMMER HAS ENDED FOR ANOTHER YEAR!

A Great and Mighty Nation

what a great and mighty nation
that can fight to eradicate
wrongs and evil
defend itself in the world
then rebuild and feed the people
in the very nations
that waged the war

what a great and mighty nation
that allows the
"tired, poor and huddled masses"
to come to its shores
to live and practice their own beliefs
and become successful
what a great and mighty nation
that can enslave a people
then overcome that misguided path
to elect a president from that very race

to lead and guide it to a
better place

what a great and mighty nation that
offers hope and inspiration to the world
its virtue, its people
their love of freedom and equality,
for each other
and all mankind
what a great and mighty nation

AMERICA

Senior Ocean Picnic

Like a silver haired flash mob
they wobbled and weaved
coming up the stairs
and over the dune
gasping for breath
carrying lawn chairs
blankets, coolers
and a diverse number of bundles

They looked somewhat like
Hannibal's army crossing
the Alps without the
elephants

Dressed in a rainbow of
Bermuda shorts
faded Hawaiian shirts
sparkling bling
floppy hats and the
latest style in sun glasses

They were a senior
style show in the making
Laughing and talking
like high schoolers playing
hooky on springs
first warm day,
their voices mingled with

the calls of seagulls
and terns
The tables spread out
laden with food
wine and bahama-mamma drinks

Laughter mingles with
the sound of crashing waves
bringing back memories
none of us
want to part with ....

Who Are We?
(the folks of OV)

We are often retired firefighters,
teachers, housewives
Doctors, lawyers, business owners
And many more

But who are we?

We play sports like
Swimming, tennis, golf, bocce ball
Shuffleboard, pickle ball
And a whole lot more

But who are we?

We go to church
Bible study
Get spiritual at the ocean
Pray for grand kids
And sing inspiring songs

But who are we?

We socialize
Go to fine restaurants
Eat hot dogs and chips
Attend movies and plays

But who are we?

We live together
In a beautiful garden
In houses, condos,
and Towers
Guards close the gates behind us
With walls around us
We are safe At night

But who are we?

are we like flocks
Of birds going south
Or giant herds on the Serengeti
All traveling the same way
All heading into the future

But who are we?

We are traveling alone
Yet all together
Maybe we should
Talk about

Who we are?

The Pop-Top Camper

I've always liked pop-top campers
they are compact,
lite and seem to fit
minimalists and wanderers

Oh, they have their problems:
cold, no jons, wind buffeted
bears can enter with one swipe,
and they lack the style and class
upper folks so enjoy

but you can back them into
the smallest of spots and
get to chum with
everyday folks

it's a wonder of technology
that is simple to employ
and gives days full laughter,
excitement and joy

listening to neighbors most
intimate conversations
coming through canvas,
sand in the sheets
all free when pop topping!

But the pop tops most
venerable attribute
(besides gas mileage supreme)
is hearing the birds,
enjoying the fresh air
and hearing nuts fall on your roof

you put them up
you take them down and
store them in the garage

they are called campers
not RVs or motorhomes
cruisers or fifth wheels!

no one wants a s'more in
or near a motor home!
too much sticky on the walls!
Kids are too messy to
motor home in the wild
but just the right age to camp in
pop tops!

What's Your Name?

(I knew it yesterday!)

You look so very familiar
As you suddenly appear

Did we go to school together?
Do your kids play with mine?

I think it's Janet or is it Jane
Your husband is a lawyer?
Or is your name Sawyer?

I dare not say a name I'm not sure of
It could be Jim or is it Jerry?
They look somewhat alike

And so I choose from a list
Of dubious, mumbled greetings
I have prepared for this aging mind
I use them more and more everyday!

Hello friend
Hi bro
Hey dude
Good to see you buddy
What's happening neighbor
What you been up to fella
Hey girlfriend
Hi sweetie

Hello pretty lady
Greetings kiddo
Where have you been lately
Hello stranger
Long time no see
What bring you into this store

Or in desperation with
hopes I'll get a first name, too
"What is your last name again?"

At which time "Smith" comes popping out
And I still won't know
the first name !!!

Read Them Louder One More Time!

Chapter Nine

Why We Hold Hands

to greet each other
to cross a street
to comfort a friend
to read one's palm
to play poker

to keep your hands warm
to keep children close
to keep from tripping
to say, "I'm here"
to keep someone from falling over a cliff

when helping someone out of a hole
when playing London Bridges
when playing crack the whip
when manicuring your nails
when doing a lake search

to keep from getting lost
on dates with those we like
at the altar when we say forever
when we say I love you
so we won't be scared
the older we get
the more we hold hands
to tell our spouse we are alive
and love you

I think God will
hold our hand for
all eternity

Will you let me hold yours?

Flowers for my Love

Flowers for my love
I just can't decide

Daffodils - $4.95
Sunflowers - $7.99
Mixed bouquet - $12.59
Premium bouquet -$ 16.59
Dozen roses $19.99

Each day you kiss me and
in the darkest deepest night
when the blankets from my shoulders fall
you tuck me in so tenderly
(I'm really not sleeping !)

You've changed so many diapers
fed the cat every day
when I felt weak you lifted me up
bought me gifts we could not afford
listened to my pontificating,
wandering thoughts until the wee
hours of the morning
you've told me every day
You think I'm wonderful
and will love me for ever

Today I will buy all the bouquets of flowers!!
and a box of choice chocolates, too!!

Daffodils go in the bathroom
Sunflowers in the library
Premium bouquet to the front widow
Mixed bouquet on the dining room table
A dozen roses placed a single rose at a time
in each and every room
the garage
the kitchen
the shower
you have said you love me,
I love you in return

Chocolates
eat one every day

Love expresses itself
with the first cup of coffee every morning
just for you
and I wrote these words
just for you

Beauty

there
may
be
more
beautiful
people
in
this
world
but
the
most
beautiful
to
me
tis
you
and
to
you
tis
me

Flowers and Candy

The candy is dandy
the flowers were handy

I drove extra miles
'cause I remember your smile

though it may sound sappy
you make me so happy

the candy's a treat
to show you are sweet

the flowers so fair
show you I care

so this little gift
I hope will give you a lift

It could have been a toy
because you bring so much joy

the real reason
in any season
is what I'll carve on a tree
and hope you agree

I LOVE YOU!

Janet's Song
(Dedicated to Janet Young, Ocean Village Florida)

my voice is silent now -
I use my eyes to
Show the depth
Of my love

My hands - they move
But I cannot control the
space and shape they take

My arms can no longer
Reach, hug, or even clap with joy
A wheelchair holds
My legs

But this hasn't
Taken the beauty
Of life's wonder away
my
smile shows what my
Heart wants to say,
That Life is good

I know You hear the
beating and pounding

Of my heart
Saying

I will love you forever

A Jesus Moment

She had just stolen a purse
from an old helpless lady
She was young and on a bicycle

A struggling an unemployed
black girl in a white world
pinned to the ground by
a Jimmy Jon's delivery boy
and other helpful citizens

"I'm trying to get to California
to get a new start
a new life!"
she pleaded in hand cuffs
A jail sentence awaited

I looked into her eyes and
saw her fright and terror
Do I just see her crime
Compliment the crime stoppers
Or try to come to terms
With her poverty and distress

A time for my core values to step forward

"Help me to be aware and help those who are so needy"
I prayed last week in church

The watching crowd
annoyed, distracted from Art Prize
quickly returned to hanging bobbles and
paintings of Jesus on the cross

If Tomorrow Should Never Come

Hey good buddy!
If tomorrow should never come
and today is the
everlasting end of all time
I will forever walk
through all of eternity
remembering our
friendship
good times
friends and
work

Our philosophizing life's mysteries
over wine and good music

We laughed, got silly and
enjoyed life too much
(can one do that?)

We did some charity work and
shared our days, helped our brothers
drank a few and
thanked our God for
giving us time here on earth

If tomorrow should never come
today and yesterday were enough to
make our journey have

special meaning
a memory to carry us through all time
a life worth living
The world has met many
a character and saint
but you and I
are special wanderers
we questioned everything
A trophy awaits I'm sure!!

Poetry in Heaven

Will there be poetry in Heaven

Many love race cars
and hope the streets of gold
are black with tire treads
smoke and squealing tires

Some love quilting
and hope celestial clotheslines
flutter inside the pearly gates
with colorful patterned quilts

The lovers of fishing and animal trophies
mounted on mansion walls
just seems out of place

Some want their epithets
in stone transported from
overgrown country cemeteries
brought inside the pearly gates
engraved with degrees and countries visited
They might find the angels unimpressed

But me thinks the poets
who bring a rhyme or two
and words which shaped the world should
have a chance with
angels, saints and others

who might listen to
my poem...
"This love I bring to Heaven's door
It warmed our
hearts on earth below
it's all we had when
life moved on through
cloudy days
and happy"

Grandpa Where is Heaven

Grandpa, where is heaven?
Is it in the stars
beyond the horizon
hidden by the moon
or in some faraway galaxy?

Sweet child, I know where heaven is
and you will too
You will see glimpses of it
as you walk through your life

It is where love is.
You will see it everyday
with every little good thing and
act of kindness you do

it is wherever
Grandma is and you are

How far away is heaven?
How far away are you and Grandma from me?
Love is in our hearts
so it is just an inch or two away
Put your hand over your heart
and feel God's love beating
in your soul.

It's where tomorrow is
where you'll find the
poor eating dinner with the rich
and people of all colors and races
loving each other

My Body is my Scrapbook

(Dedicated to Paula who gave me this metaphor)

My body is a scrapbook
Not only housing my DNA
passed down from grandparents in
Germany / Netherlands
but scars from every bump
bruise and fall
I've ever taken

The childhood swings,
monkey bars and slides
produced chipped teeth
and left bruises and scars
some on the inside
some on the outside

Every operation has left
lines and indentations
which remind me of times
I would like to forget

Aches and pains
in joints and bones
remind me of old football injuries
and body slams by players
much bigger than me

My brain is like a tape
recorder filled with
memories of
every fish I have ever caught,
my first kiss
adventures in the woods
certificates, degrees and awards
and all those hours
in the classroom

Burn marks and animal bites
from long ago are
still visible on arms and legs
Grandkids want to know what
they mean and where did I get them
(I exaggerate a bit - I must admit)
(episodes with bears and skunks the most common)

In every scrapbook
there are the
special
intriguing items
hidden away

In my body scrapbook
those are found in my heart

The things I store there
I remember the most vividly
and visit whenever possible

It was the pounding of my heart
When you said,
"yes, I'd love to!"
when I asked for that first date.
The sun-filled day when you
answered my question

"Will you marry me?"
With a resounding, "Yes !"

And now
It's the
"I will be with you forever"
That brings sunshine into everyday!
A scrapbook body
That's not too shoddy

Thoughts About Weather

Trees sweep and brush
Against The sky to keep it clean

Ocean waves push and shove
Against the shore
To pile the dunes
and stack the sand

Snow blankets
The fields and woods
To keep them warm
Until the early spring

Rain falls from the heavens
To wash the mountains
And fill the streams and lakes

Storms chase people
Into houses
To let them see and hear
God's awesome power

The sun shines
To grow the grass and give us hope

Weather gives
folks topics for conversations
And predictions which
never seem to end

It's raining here, what's it doing there?

Our Old Barn

The universe of farm life
begins and meets in the barn
like galaxies converge
near black holes
and supernovas

The cows in the barn chewing their cud
enjoying earlier meals
from meadows and spring fields
horses licking foam from lips
whipped across salt licks
delicious beyond belief

Chickens laying eggs
for Easter,
pies and omelets
and maybe an occasional fox

Pigeons cooing
sweet melodies
of peace toward all
until the hawk comes near

Mice boring into haylofts
stacked high with summer hay
daring the fat old cat
to come and chase him

And sparrows chasing
wheat chaff
carried upward on
heated cow flatulence

This is where I enter
with doors squeaking
dim lights and barnyard smells
cows waiting utters full

The barn is getting old
and none of them know
that I'm leaving for college soon
and without paint
and repair this barn
their universe
will soon just be another black hole

Where Do Socks Go

It only seems fair that as
A poet of little distinction
And questionable fame
That I should take a crack
At where socks go

I have heard stories
From wives, daughters and grandkids
Of socks that magically disappear
In dryers new and old

Some were tossed in
To be roaming free
Others tied in simple knots
The knot remains in only one sock
The other not to be seen

Some pinned together
Pin still closed
One sock not to be found

Mothers, wives, detergent junkies
Laundry experts and even a priest
all have theories

Hung up in shirt sleeves
caught in lint traps
Laundry fairies

Gremlins, under the bed
And one even involved a queen
But still only one sock remains
So I thought about physics
Magical soap
And Agatha Christi mysteries

Confused and without
Answers
I struggled and thought

I finally asked
A small girl of only eight
"Honey, where do socks go?"

She laughed and said,
"Grandpa have you ever
Checked the bathroom!"
(Get it? You go in the bathroom)

My Last Book

I often wonder
who will buy
my last book
my last poetry book that exists on earth

I'd have been gone for many years
In heaven playing senior tennis and golf
maybe reading psalms

My daughters
would have given away the
last of my books years ago

Great, great grandkids who probably
have had reading chips placed in their brains
have no need for books

So there was only one
book left of all I had written
It's In a garage sale
battered and torn

A young man in a hurry
buys it as a gift on the way
to a retirement home to visit
a failing parent

After having several poems read to them
with failing memory and loss of sight
the parent says to the son
"I would like to have met the author!"

This is the way I'd like my books history to end!

Amish for a Day

Today on wobbly bicycle
I rode the Pumpkin Vine Trail
through Amish country Indiana

Cows grazing close on every side
neat white farmhouses
with laundry on the clotheslines
men plowing in the fields

Stately carriages pulled
by well-groomed horses
men in straw hats
women in prayer caps
Simple yet elegant

I became Amish in my mind
for just a moment upon the trail
The sleek and shining horses
were mine
I knew their names

The foals and colts
I would not brag
but felt the joy
as my little children
ran them round

The sun was shining bright
The fields were green and growing
Ascension Thursday was being celebrated
I felt the presence of God all around
I'm Amish today, Lord
and all is well

Reflecting on a Last Paddle

Would I want to know
if this were to be my
last paddle?

Would I paddle slower to
watch the darting fish more closely
Would I listen more intently to the
drips fall off my paddle as I
drew it through the water?

Would I breathe in more deeply
and fill my lungs more completely
enjoying the lingering night smells and
the crisp morning air seasoned
with dogwood and apple blossoms?

Would I watch the browsing
deer until they disappeared
into the trees?

Would I fall asleep under a bright and
glowing moon in a chair
with a bed nearby?

The last paddle may come with
our knowledge or not

I think not knowing is my choice

When I Thought You Might Die

no room for terror
this is something worse
terror goes away in the bright sun light
this happens to others
does not happen in my world
badly shaken
like air being sucked out of a room
there is no way to open a window
feeling of being hollow
being detached from my body
the suddenness
you are here still in space
but yet not here
feeling so fragile
could do something outside normal boundaries
without any inhibitions
like cry in the park
all the future is squeezed into the numbness of this moment
a feeling of helplessness
people from another dimension are reaching into yours to help

they are like news stories
out there
can't reach the emptiness you feel
a feeling of seasickness
it reaches into every part of your life

eating, sleeping, past, present, future
it possesses your mind and body
joy and happiness are gone

children singing songs is like a candle
experiences with death, the candle is blown out
children with hollow expressions
look through rain-streaked windows
too sad to cry

Do Dogs Go to Heaven

Kids probably ask the question first
days after they get
their first puppy
parents answer quickly
so sure of their response

We give them special names
like King, Mercedes and Rover
We name trees and fish after them
even a child's favorite food is a dog

Dogs often get their own house
their own special food
prepared in pretty dishes
even their poop is picked up wherever they go

After thinking for a while...
if dogs go to heaven
shouldn't cats go to heaven also?
Will there be enough
room for all these creatures?

To discuss these facts
seems like opening
a can of worms
and speaking of worms...

Slowly Reading Poems While Walking Home

Chapter Ten

A Poem for Walking Home

I used to think of home
as the place where I started life
later as a place where
I grew up

For a while I thought of home as
parents, brothers and sisters
Eventually
my school, community,
synagogue and church

And as I matured
I thought of home
as my nation and the world
and finally all people as my brothers and sisters
All life that lives in the universe...
even life yet to be yet to be discovered

As I aged
I thought of home as maybe a
place in the future
an eternal home

So now I am walking toward wherever my next Home will be
Who should I walk with
I don't want to walk the final miles alone

so I choose to walk with all
my earthly brothers and sisters
and most of all YOU

I want to walk home with YOU
Wherever you are going
I want to be there too

Caught in Yesterday

Yesterday was so certain
routines established
we worked hard to find
middle ground with spouse and friends

The path was clear
we walked it often
knew it by memory
no major decisions to attempt

Yesterday was comfortable
like childhood nursery rhymes
our hard-earned goals and opportunities
established

like a spider's web
it holds and ensnares us in the past
But sometimes
While praising and reliving the past
Yesterday's efforts let us see the present clearly
And so today we surge ahead

We try to meet new friends
experience new adventures
Attend a church of a different faith ...

Hopefully, today is more a bit of tomorrow
than yesterday ...

How I Start my Day

I can choose
How to start my day

TV with news and
Pretty weather girl

iPad with Facebook and
catching up on my mail

Being retired
I can choose to stumble
around in the early morning
taking extra time getting dressed
Or even design to get up at noon

I remember how dad
Used to start his day
Same as he finished his day
A prayer on his knees by the bed

I can also choose what to think about
As I start my day

I can relive yesterday's news
Or get a jump on tasks I have to do

I can start to worry
About bills, war, maybe even politics

Over the years I have collected
A number of things that help me get
A good start to the day

A cup of coffee in a dimly lit room
Listing 5 to 10 reasons why I'm grateful
A brief prayer for those hurting and in need
A promise to do a random act of kindness today

And a joke to make me smile
"Why did the bee get married?
Because he found his honey."

A 2nd cup of coffee and
BRING ON THE NEW DAY!

A Transformagical Moment

In the deep woods
the whispering harmony
of stringed instruments
floats effortlessly
through the trees
like cottonwood on a spring breeze
or wandering butterflies
softly gliding over
mats of moss and white pine needles

towering pine trees
bursting with cones
lean over to listen
wanting to take in each melody
fearful of missing even one note

players with nimble fingers
move their bodies effortlessly to the
light airy tunes
magical sounds spring from
string and bow

it is then a gentle
humming is heard and
voice are added
first from one player than another
they unite with string, drum and nature

a woodsy symphony
has begun

I listen transfixed
wanting to move, dance and
live life fully in that moment
the warm embracing sun
shimmers in the moving trees
giving players and instruments
a warm glow

it is then
I know I'm in a very special place
A transformagical place!

"Why Take the Shortest Way?"

our lives are moving fast
children growing up
money to be made
lawns must be cut
retirement to plan
body pains are in full swing

so when we travel
and we live our shortening lives
is it always best
to take the shortest way?

just for once and
just for today
on my homeward route
I had a large latte
stopped by a schoolyard and
watched the children play

I took the longer way home
and thought about
Socrates, Jesus
Plato and Buddha

I wonder if they always
took the shortest
way home?

When You are Away

When you are away
There are empty spots
Throughout the house and
my day but most of all
my heart

The chair you sit in
The bed you make warm
The coffee pot sits half full
Your empty cup on the counter

The hamper
Stuffed with dirty clothes
I don't smell your perfume
or hear you putting dishes,
well-organized, in the dishwasher

My Conversations
echo back to me and
fall dead upon the walls and floors

But most of all
I feel emptiness
within my soul that
you fill so easily with
your smile
gentle touch and
conversations that delight

So when you are done
helping and sharing your life,
kindness, and smile with those in need
return to me
and fill those empty spaces
only you and you alone can fill

Today

I'm going through today
Perhaps in an airplane, car
on a bike or even walking

Sometimes sitting in my chair
looking over my shoulder
at yesterday
squinting ahead to see tomorrow

In today's moments I savor
food, fun, friendships
And service

Would life be better
to do more or less today

I guess I will hold my breath
until I gasp
and breath in the now

Today is the now
It's all I have
the air is good
I hear my breath
and this is where life Is lived
one moment at a time

Thinking About Being Happy

How can I be happy
if I don't know what it is

Is a child's happiness
the same as an adult

Is happiness
the lack of problems and stress

Can happiness
be shared and passed to others

Can one part of me be happy
while another part is sad

Can I start down the road to happiness
with just a happy thought

I think I'm happiest
when I'm with you

Would you spend more time with me
so I'm happy more often

If we make each other happy
we could start a happiness movement

I'm happy I shared this with you

Partners

Trustworthy, loyal and spiritually connected
peace and harmony are important
to this delicate and fragile
thing we know as marriage
Of all the relationships in marriage
Partner is not the one most often highlighted
Lover's the one usually written about
Soul mate's given recognition
Parenthood glorified
Breadwinner important

However to me after
much thought and deliberation
I feel Partnership
a most worthy attribute
Sharing equally parenting, housework
all the big decisions of life

The Bible and other holy books seem to give
one partner more control in the relationship
However in modernity
With logic and the divine blessing of a long life
Equal partnership gives marriage
It's most glorious honor
And may one understand all marriages,
even gay marriages
It's not who you choose
It's who you are that makes all the difference

spider webs

spider webs hang in the garage
under the deck
between bushes
above the porch
behind bedroom doors
in living rooms corners and
eventually cover everything
even my laptop has the web

in the morning sun light
they are beautiful
in the afternoon sun
geometrically exquisite
in the entry way at night
yucky for guests to feel and see

they lay in wait
capturing insects and floating air debris
in early times used as bandages
they are natures
thing of beauty or frustration

but for me
I think I spun one many years ago
to capture you
a beautiful butterfly flying by
and now each web I see
I pause and think of you

if I remember right you were a monarch
in a yellow angora sweater
or were you a busy bee !

(love is often found unexpectedly in nature)

Wine Before Dinner

A nervous stomach
I told the doctor
I just cannot eat my evening meal
With thoughtful deliberation
he prescribed
a glass of wine to settle
that nervous stomach before I ate my food

Being a good Christian
and not a drinker
I thought I knew just what to do

I took a tumbler from the cupboard and
filled it to the brim with
nice red wine
and slowly drank my prescription down

I feel "loopy"
I told my spouse
He said, "You did what?"

The good Christian
that he is said,
"I'm too ashamed to bless this meal"

So that night
I ate an unblessed meal
with a settled stomach and giddy conversation!

It was delicious!

Ocean Village

colorful hibiscus
beautiful bougainvillea
hedges manicured to perfection
swept green tennis courts
sky blue pools
softly waving palms
pelicans riding thermals into
sapphire blue skies
Then there is the beauty of all
the wrinkles faces
tennis players with leg braces
golfers with arm wraps
folk walking with limps
white and silver hair bikers
seniors holding hands

friends reminiscing over
coffee at the Tiki
...yeah, the pool was filled with sand
after the hurricane!
...remember when Father Joe
blessed the motorcycles at "Arts Cheese" restaurant
...How about when the barge sank by the jetty?
Were there square groupies on board?"

But it was at the Inn
on prime rib night
when you said

"Ocean Village is beautiful, but you
my love are gorgeous"

Thoughts About Rainy Weather

reservoirs fill
tired golf muscles heal
tennis courts rest
husbands talk longer with wives
bird poo gets washed off statues
lawns get free watering
writers have more time to write
stores sell backlogs of umbrellas
children get puddles to splash in
library books get read
rivers and streams get to roar
pigs get to roll in the mud
ducks get to show off their diving skills
lawn sprinklers sleep
twigs and leaves get to go with flow
robins get more night crawlers
golf greens relax from hackers
ministers dig up sermons on Noah's Ark
Beall's sell more rain coats
roofers get the day off
windows get rain streaked
folks at OV get to talk about the flood of 2014
and you get to read this and
wish that Jerry didn't have your e-mail!

remember rainbows
only come after the rain!

The Joy of Being an Adult

It really isn't a problem
Being an adult
I smile at folks who struggle
With the "empty nest"

What's the problem
A full refrigerator,
a quiet house
Your lazy boy just to yourself?

Having just entertained
A two and six-year-old over Christmas,
The patter of "little feet" is
far overrated

Stumbling over toys
Being buzzed by drones
having a "children's table"
Little Emily burping up her squash
(or is it mashed carrots)
On grandpa's new shirt!
And playing far too many games of "Sorry"
All without a nap!
Being an adult is a joy!

I can finally make
decisions by myself like
drinking beer and
watching football
Now I just have to stay awake to do them

The Remembrance Garden

Of all the special places at Ocean Village -
mesmerizing ocean
croaking ponds
lush golf greens
clay tennis courts and
dining excellence at the Inn

my special place
to be alone is
The Remembrance Garden

I take my shoes off
and walk upon
each weathered brick

I read slowly the words
that aching hearts
composed about those that were
loved and cherished
I feel tears on my soul
for their friends and family

I say to each who passed
how loved they were
and even though
we never met
they left behind
a wonderful legacy of

friends and family
who treasured them
And so good folks
who have gone before -
Thanks for being you!
It won't be long and we will join you

A Fire Poking Stick

About half the people in the world
love poking fires and
irritating burning wood

They can't leave a
beautifully built fire
fall in on itself

Fires built with precision
hold no special place in
their world view

Every fire's purpose seems to be
an object to be poked and prodded
into a more sparkling
glowing mass
If it burns faster, great!

They glance around each new campsite
looking for the perfect poking stick
short skinny ones won't do
you need long strong limbs
even a golf club will do as a last resort
fire pokers have even been known to use
hot dog forks!

No one knows how they got this way
I think the reason for these fire pokers is

in their early youth they got coal in
their stocking for Christmas!

Trash Talk

No one in good standing
writes a poem about
trash

So I guess it's up to me
To write something
trashy

Reviewers trash bad movies
We tell our kids not to
"Trash the place"
When having friends over
there's trash talk in sports

There's a trash container in
every room
We throw things on the trash heap
We carry out the trash
We smash stuff in the
trash compactor or
Burn it in an incinerator

Some folks have trashy minds
They read trashy novels
Look down on trailer trash
Think they are better than white trash
but
think trashy girls are more fun!

If you are getting tired of
all this trash talk
And think this is getting a
Little trashy
Maybe you should
get some fresh air

But don't ball up this poem and
Throw it in the trash!!

Life's Special Moments

Often
When a grandpa and grandson
Try something
For the very first time
A special moment occurs in which
A grandson learns
What he can become
And
Grandpa can relive
His childhood's past
While
helping shape his
grandson's future
best of all
a bond is formed
which they will forever share
In their own
Private world

Ice Cream Sundays

Many folks like
Ice cream
but I think kids
and fun people
enjoy it the most

Just the mention
of a possible cone
or especially a sundae
and they get all giddy
start to bounce on the balls of their feet
talk faster
and smile like a Cheshire

When eating a sundae
they swirl the creamy mixture
to tickle their palate
and have their own special way
to savor each bite

When done come the
reviews and exhortations
plans for more sundaes
maybe tomorrow
or even to night!

What is it about sundaes
that makes them so happy?
I think I should have one
just to find out!!

When I Am with You

Do you hear the owl?
I'm not afraid when I'm with you, Grandpa

Was that a wolf or the neighbor's dog?
Grandpa I'm not afraid!
I'm with you!

I hear a large branch breaking.
Could that be a bear?
Oh grandpa, there aren't bears around here
and besides I'm with you!

Grandma must never
be afraid because she's
with you all the time!

Grandpa,
I will never be afraid
because you will always be
in my heart and with me for ever
and I will be with you
in case you are ever afraid...

I love you grandpa
I love you too, Jackie

conversations from the hot tub with
a four-year-old

Still Walking and Wondering

Chapter Eleven

Pancakes for Dinner

Maybe it was nostalgia
Or just a grandparents sweet tooth
But when I grandpa suggested
Pancakes for dinner
Grandma didn't refuse
I stirred the batter
And dropped in the eggs
I felt the long gone grandkids pushing
Shoving, "let me flip them" they clamored,
I know they weren't there
But still I had their memories
Etched deep in my soul
"They got out the syrup, butter and jam"
And flipped and tumbled the golden brown pancakes
Some on the grill
Some on the stove
Little ones as samples" Angie implored"
Jack asked for "Mickey Mouse faces"
I made them all that glorious meal
With a big pumpkin
"For grandma they yelled!"
Pancakes for dinner

Lots of butter and
Aunt Jemima syrup
Not good for the diet, but good for the soul!

The Refugees

They come cross our borders at night
some at the misty light of dawn

struggling over fences
fighting off guards with dogs
carrying crying, exhausted infants
hungry with tattered clothes

In their homeland some were
doctors, nurses, teachers
farmers and skilled workers

Now they are in enclosures
Soldiers ply them with questions

Are you Christian?
Have you been to west Africa in the last six months?
Are you gay?

Should we ask them
Do you believe in open carry?
Would you vote for a Mormon for president?

Would you drink coffee at Christmas in a totally red cup?

It's not easy being a refugee...

Reflections on Today

as I wandered
today on the golf course
with old and new friends
I tried to
live in the moment and
enjoy brightness of the day

struggled with a few bad swings
felt exhilaration of other's
wonderful shots so near the pin
but yet no birdies

friendly ribbing
caring for each other
tasty hot dogs
popcorn
Coke and beer

I took it in at every
opportunity
there I was in the moment
I hated to feel its end

so as I parted
I breathed it all In
filled my lungs
with cigar smoke

and as I
coughed and sneezed
murmured let’s do this again
now I'm home reflecting
reliving those sacred moments

Why wouldn't that damn ball
just drop in !!

An Esoteric Poem

I tried to write
an esoteric poem
an erudite extraction
of thoughts
and words
which would
be an obscure mystery
an existential
extrusion of space and time
a polemic
of those who
write with certainty
which might include
pre Cambrian
Continental drift theory
but it became abstruse
cryptic and heavy
which I guess
makes this an esoteric
poem!

Journeys

The greatest journeys that
Lie before us
aren't necessarily
Following goat herder paths from
2000 years ago

Reading about Saints wandering on self-help expeditions
Into the wilderness
Sailing on cruise ships laden with food

Or perhaps checking off bucket lists of wild adventures

Maybe our greatest journey
should be walked slowly
back into our souls

Remembering our first contact with
the purpose
of why we are here
quiet reflection
serving

Living simply
A day of sunshine
Holding a needy hand

Dad's Old Guns

If dad were still here
I'm sure he would cringe at
the way I'm sending the
sporting implements of
joy and delight from his youth
to be melted
taken from this world
Hopefully then used for toys,
trucks and more

The guns I see and
read about today
do not put food on the table or
defend against beasts that attack or
armies that invade

They accidentally kill the innocent
take the life of an animal for sport
to be mounted over the fireplace
or family room wall

Some guns are used to intimidate
others are used to impress friends
they say they're needed for self-defense
but often a human is killed in the
heat of an argument

I don't think God put his creatures on
Earth to be killed for sport

I know dad would say
"Son, they are yours to enjoy"
So I'm putting them away forever
to make this world
a little less dangerous place.

I'm sure he would get a bang out of this

Our Personal Big Bang Theory

In 1965 the big bang theory
About the origin of the universe
was confirmed

Now I'm thinking
About each of our personal
Big Bang discovery theories

When did each of us
Discover our place in the world
Then the universe

Or maybe we haven't found it yet
We are still looking
Asking the questions

discovering who we are
Where we are
Why we are

Focusing on our final destination
What we travel for
and toward

giving us ontological purpose
The echoes of our origins
Getting louder the older we grow

Ssenlufdnim

I decided to look
backwards for a while

even the title
of this work
is "mindfulness" spelled backwards

I wanted to drag
the present into the past
there are so many
good things about the past

I looked younger
had more hair
my clothes weren't as old

I hit the golf ball further
the tennis ball harder
walked a little faster

in the past
yesterday's expectations
are now being lived
in the present

in the present

Mindfulness
comes in shorter breaths,
breathing in less but
listening more deeply
meditation a daily desire

however
it's hard to drag
the present into the past
or the future

so I'll just think about
this beautiful moment I'm in...
I'm very lucky to be
sharing it with you!

Have You Ever Wondered

Have you ever wondered why
so many people speak for God?

The pope speaks ex cathedra
Mohammed wrote his conversations with God in a book
Preachers say God speaks through them
Some folks say they talk to God every day
Musicians sing about god walks, and talks with them

And what about all those holy books?
The authors state they
had epiphanies, dreams, burning bushes
and visions of God

Many religions say God only
communicates through
males

And religion often instructs men what
women should wear
and when to talk and
when to be silent

Many speakers for God say
they have been given special signs
even golden tablets
with rules and commandments
for all others to follow

Even those in other cultures who
have never heard of these Books or prophets
Others don't say it's God
speaking to them
but departed relatives
and spirits from the past

Occasionally folks go to heaven
and come back like
the boy who has a bestselling book
about his time in heaven

It could be heresy but
some believe that
God talks to everyone equally

Most of those who say they
have that special relationship with
God are making money from that connection

And if you are wondering,
yes
I think God told me to write this verse ...

Life is Too Busy

Before I start today
I need to finish yesterday
Maybe I packed too much into it
But there are things unfinished
I wanted
needed and
just had to do

Now they wait
In nervous piles
like last week's laundry
Things seem to move so fast

I'm not sure I had time to
enjoy my lunch
have a bit of fun
I don't remember if I smiled or
Took time to pet the cat

I hurried through every part of the day
Even my breaks and happy hour

I need to push the pause button
Take a deep breath ...
And Finish yesterday

The Obituaries

the obituaries
it's Sunday
and I'm reading the obituaries
the older I get the more
I'm drawn to read them
they are so interesting and intriguing

I first look to see if
my name is there
it makes me feel more alive
when I'm not listed!

then I check for friends
for some odd reason
most folks want to outlive their friends
competition to the very end!

next I look for folks my
age or younger
inside we think our good life choices
Let us live longer than our friends
yea me!

then I look at older looking faces
and think how beautiful
they must have been in youth

occasionally I will read an obituary
from top to bottom

to give respect and credit
to a life well lived

I hope ten years from now
I don't spend my whole Sunday reading obituaries
I think I'm getting
so good at obituaries I may write my own

when I do
I'll insist on using my
high school graduation picture
cause I think I was
damn good looking!

The Bucket Lists

I have my bucket list
and thought I would ask
Perfecto a father of 4,
little kids recently arrived from Mexico)
who was working on our condo lawn
if he would grab his bucket list
and walk with me for one day
we could talk about our bucket lists
he said wasn't just sure what a bucket list was

I came with a sturdy metal bucket
he brought a small plastic one
like those kids use for trick or treat

I'm thinking of buying a corvette
it would be great I suggested
the wind in my hair and all

he asked if it would be safe to park it
on the street at night
many of the street lights are out he said

I guess he didn't know I had several garages
then I told him
I've always wanted a fifth wheel
after describing a fifth wheel
I explained I want to travel
the back roads of America

he said he had traveled
many to get here
and most are dusty
without available water, and had lots of unleashed dogs

what's on your list I inquired?
a green card he suggested

is that an e-co friendly greeting card
I asked
I really had never seen one

he also suggested he
would like to move to a safer neighborhood
with a school
his kids could walk to

I could sense
our bucket lists were somewhat different
but thought I'd list at least
another item
"I'd like to take a month long cruise"
he smiled and said
he had never seen the ocean
he didn't know much about ships
but his brother had worked
in a ships kitchen for several years
it was then I got to thinking
maybe instead of
a bucket list ,

I could make basket list
a picnic basket list of ideas
to help others achieve their
bucket lists
Helping
folks like Perfecto
would be my bucket list !

Thoughts About Getting Old

Tomorrow's shadows
are beginning to cloud today's
expectations

Yesterday's achievements don't
bring as much joy today as they did yesterday

This fragile moment
I stand in
is on shaky legs

I try to gather
The past, present and future
into this moment

I find my mind Looking for
Meaning in little children's wonder

They're having fun riding by on tricycles
People walking pampered dogs
And find myself repeating Sunday school songs
I know I'm finding the best in life in
Old friends
Good wine
mingled memories
And hope for sunshine tomorrow

Running Too Fast

We all know and hope
we will walk slowly through
this journey we call life
However daily life gets so busy
we get walking and talking fast
and running hell-bent
toward the future

Even in retirement
there are sports to be played
restaurants to be visited
coupons to be used
sales to attend
new friends to be meet
religious requirements that must be met

One day we will realize
We must slow down

I think taking time to smell the flowers
is based in the deep psychological need

For self-actualization
and especially picking a few flowers
While smelling them
to share with shut-ins and friends

Today I may try to step off
the pseudo treadmill life has become
I'm going to try to sit a while under a shade tree
call a few of my unvisited friends
send some flowers
reread my resolutions and bucket list
most of all slow down

Or I could run right past
The most important things in life

The Colonoscopy

Its time is here ...
I thought it was farther in the future
maybe the second coming or
global warming would have to be deal with first

at the pharmacy the giant container and
bag of prescriptions were waiting
Drawing knowing glances and looks of sympathy

I heard a child ask his mother
"He has to drink all of that in three days?"
"No," she answered, "In three hours!"
"YUCK!
I don't want to grow up!"

The five days without vegetables
Wasn't bad, but I tired quickly of
Jell-O and applesauce.

It could've been my imagination,
but I thought my spouse was especially noisy
When eating popcorn, peanuts and
Hershey bars with almonds!
During this stretch
I sure wasn't looking forward
to the clear diet day
I looked hard for egg and bacon Jell-O
Or cinnamon bun broth

The three-hour drinking task is
just about here
my spouse says
"I think I'll order a pizza since
You will be busy during dinner."

The chance of us
both being in the hospital
at the same time
is a real possibility!

What to Wear in Heaven

Have you ever wondered
What people will wear in heaven?

I'm thinking bikinis are out
with all that sunshine folks could get burned
burqas would create too
much laundry for the angels
men wouldn't need overalls
because they won't have to work
I don't even think men have to wear ties,
at least I have never seen pictures of the saints wearing them
the Bible states that children and babies will be there
I hope there won't be diapers though

Speaking of that
I just read an article that
90 % of all religions think dogs will be in heaven
you really don't think there will be doggy bags
along the streets of gold, do you?

Maybe just maybe
we will each be able to wear one favorite
piece of clothing from earth
perhaps a baseball hat with our
political party logo or NRA hats
they would help newcomers make conversation
I'm not so sure about tattoos and
body piercings though

If they do allow clothing
I'm sure our bathrobes would do just fine
besides, we older folks have already spent
most of our time in them!

My Final Resting Place

Some are buried at sea
but I would find it hard to breathe there
Others go in drawers as ashes
I would feel like underwear in there

How about an urn on a fireplace mantel?
I'd be afraid they'd drop me while dusting
and under the old oak in the back forty
would seem so lonely

Those who died with valor and honor
lay in Arlington
Some pass and no one knows
where they lie
A famous few are said to
go straight to heaven

At one time
I thought I might like to lie
beneath a children's playground
and hear the running of feet
and shrieks of laughter every day

But I'm sure
I would tire of the
petty arguments and little fights
and all that jumping
might give me a headache

I really can't
Let my kids decide
They would take
So many votes
I'd stay in the funeral home for years

So unless
I change my mind
find some small
Country church
with the cemetery
out behind
(Protestant preferred, but
Catholic will do, I just don't know the music)
where they have too many tenors
and need a bass or two
and the sermons are short
and they have lots of potlucks
because I love the smell of homemade apple pie!

He is Gone

Just yesterday he was here
A very good friend
Just like you
And hopefully I am to you

I still hear his voice echoing in my thoughts
He will be in my mind forever
I wanted to call him just now
About the weird news I read today

We both loved reading articles
about strange folks doing goofy stuff
like taking pictures in the nude
Then we would say
"what the hell were they thinking!"

But he is gone
He took some of me with him
This cranky old friend of mine
I hope there're newspapers in the great beyond
With articles about people
Doing silly stuff,
maybe Angels dancing in bikinis on the heads of needles
For then he will remember me
And say to the astonished heavenly folks
"What the hell are they thinking?!?"

Watching for Tomorrow

I know tomorrow is coming
However I thought today
I'd wait by the sidelines
To watch it sneak in
Just once
watch it as it occurs naturally
So with a glass of wine
in evening setting sun
And solemn resolve
In silence
glancing forward and backward
I'm waiting for tomorrow to occur
often
I tried to herd it in
To be a leading force
To shape and move it around
My plans for it seem so important
Tomorrow must depend on who I am
And what my plans are for the new day
However
I just happened to glance back through today
And I see Yesterday and Tomorrow
Holding hands in today
Both like me are waiting in the shadows
Looking at what's happening today
And saying
birds will chirp
Weather will happen

I will find purpose in both
in yesterday and tomorrow

But in this moment is
where I am found ……
I will Remember yesterday
Live today
try not to worry about tomorrow
it will come
So I wait in the shadows
With Yesterday and Tomorrow
for yet another day to come…..
(however I have red wine and
a poem to keep me company)

Thoughts on Bad Behavior

I'm sure people are not bad
Just Because they disagree with me
And are not good because they do

Being rude and classless
Is really not a sin
Just difficult to live with and
Unpleasant to be around

Even being a bully often shows
Evidence of a previous sad,
Dysfunctional or painful youth

Some individuals are taught misogyny, sexism and
Homophobia as part of their religion
racism passed down from parents
with lots of ignorance mixed in

Finding the origins of bad behavior
May help to understand it but not accept it
It's when people have a choice and
yet display bad behavior
That is confusing